CHRISTIANITY AMONG THE RELIGIONS

Christianity
Among the Religions

by

E. L. ALLEN

Uno itinere non potest pervenire
ad tam grande secretum

Ruskin House

GEORGE ALLEN & UNWIN LTD

MUSEUM STREET LONDON

*Printed in Great Britain
in 12 on 13-pt Bembo type
at the University Press
Aberdeen*

PREFACE

The title of this book should be sufficient explanation of its purpose. Throughout the writing of it, I have been conscious of the debt I owe to the men and women of other lands and other faiths who have honoured me with their friendship.

E. L. ALLEN

Arana Hall
Dunedin
New Zealand

CONTENTS

Truth and Error

a. MISSION TO ISLAM

IT was in the thirteenth century that Western Christendom began to be shaken in the conviction that it possessed the absolute truth. The Church that had converted pagans, excommunicated heretics, and excluded the Jew from the common life, now found herself face to face with Islam. That enigmatic monarch Frederick II entered Jerusalem by treaty with the Sultan of Cairo and in defiance of the Pope, and the dwindling Christian principalities of Palestine took advantage of a truce with the enemy to turn against each other. Islam, it became clear, was not to be dispossessed by force of arms. The Cross and the Crescent must find some less futile and less bloody way of settling their differences. Nor was that all. For Islam had gone over to the counter-attack in the person of her philosophers. Under the patronage of the Abbasid caliphs in Baghdad, Greek medical, astronomical, and philosophical texts were translated into Arabic and commented on in the same language. Thanks to the Moslem conquest of Spain, this rich culture was carried to the gates of Western Europe. As Christian armies marched south to recover the peninsula, the new knowledge crossed the frontier in the opposite direction.

All this is part of the history of European culture. With it a new possibility emerged. There were intermediaries available who could assist in giving Averroes a Latin dress. Might not one of them be employed in rendering the same service to the Koran? Yes, if a Christian were found who wished to read it. Peter the Venerable was such a one, and in 1141 while in Spain on a tour of inspection he took the decisive step of commissioning a Latin version of the Koran. He was perhaps the first to see that it was vain to combat Islam with the sword while remaining ignorant of what it stood for. His purpose was a missionary one, and he knew that to make converts from a religion one must first study it. The Christians who undertook the task included one Robertus Retensis (of Reading?), an Englishman, but they were assisted by a Saracen of the same name as the Prophet. Robert's rendering continued in use throughout the medieval period and we shall see that it was drawn upon in particular by Nicolas of Cuas.[1]

So the missionary and not the soldier was now to be the champion of the faith. This was the bold new idea and the first Pope to espouse it was Gregory IX, though he did not for all that abandon hope that the crusading spirit might be renewed. He gave his support to the mendicant orders as they threw themselves into the enterprise. Of St Francis we know that he twice suffered disappointment before he set foot on the Holy Land. He was in Syria for more than a year (1219-1220), during which time he paid a visit to Egypt and found the crusaders there no less in need of his ministrations than the Saracens. We are told of an interview with the Sultan of Egypt, one version of which makes the latter ask for a sign that would enable him to decide between the rival religions. Another account represents the saint as offering himself to pass through fire if 'the priests of Mahomet' will do the same.[2]

Franciscans and Dominicans worked in North Africa and the Near East, sometimes meeting with martyrdom as the reward of their zeal. But the missionary needs to know the language of those to whom he goes. So in 1250 the provincial chapter of Toledo sent eight Dominicans to Tunis to study Arabic. One of them was to become famous as linguist and writer. He was Ramon Martin, whose *Pugio Fidei* was a handbook for use in

---

[1] On this subject see Ugo Monneret de Villard, *Lo Studio dell'Islām in Europa nel XII e nel XIII Secolo*, 1944.

[2] Paul Sabatier, *Vie de S. François d'Assisse*, 1920, ch. XIV.

missions to Jews as well as to Moslems.[1] Another Dominican is important for his influence on Lull. He was Ramon de Pennyafort, a Catalan by birth; he claimed to have baptized two thousand converts from Islam. It was at his instigation that Lull devoted himself to the study of Arabic, purchasing a Moorish slave to act as teacher. Largely as the result of Lull's tireless advocacy, the Council of Vienne in 1311 resolved upon the establishment of colleges for the study of Oriental languages. These were to be located at Bologna, Oxford, Salamanca, and the place of residence of the Roman court—it was necessary to be vague on that last point! Provision was to be made for their maintenance. Alas, there is no evidence that the project got beyond good intentions.

By such measures as these the stage was being set for a new kind of encounter with Islam, one based on knowledge to some extent. There was need for this, too, as one can see from a glance at some of the great preposterous opinions of Mohammed and his religion that were current at the time. Perhaps it is not surprising that Mohammed was thought of as a heretic and schismatic. In the seventh century John of Damascus, who had first-hand contact with Islam, included Mohammed in his catalogue of Christian heretics. He founded the 'Saracen' sect on the strength of a cursory acquaintance with the Scriptures and information given by an Arian monk. One story made him a priest, if not actually a cardinal! Islam was generally reputed to be an idolatrous religion with an image of Mohammed as its cult-object. Some who claimed to have visited Palestine as pilgrims declared that an image of the kind was to be seen in the Mosque of Omar. And has not the medieval morality-play given us the word 'termagant', used originally for a Moslem idol, the product of Christian ignorance and fear? [2]

[1] On Ramon Martin see *The Legacy of Islam*, 1931, pp. 272 f.
[2] For the acount of Mohammed current at the Papal Court see Matthew Paris, *Chronica Majora* (Rolls Series), iii. 343 ff. For the popular view see Dorothy Sayers' translation of *The Song of Roland*.

b. RAMON LULL

The most notable of the seventeenth-century missionaries was Ramon Lull. The words in which he expressed the ideal that governed his earlier years have often been quoted and are indeed memorable:

Many knights do I see who go to the Holy Land thinking to conquer it by force of arms. But, when I look at the end thereof, all of them are spent without attaining that which they desire. Wherefore, it appears to me, O Lord, that the conquest of that sacred land will not be achieved . . . save by love and prayer and the shedding of tears as well as blood. . . . Let the knights become religious, let them be adorned with the sign of the Cross and filled with the grace of the Holy Spirit, and let them go among the infidels to preach truth concerning thy Passion.[1]

What is less well known is that he later abandoned this ideal. In preparation for the Council of Vienne he made up his mind 'to propose three things for the honour and reverence and increase of the holy Catholic faith'. The first was study of the Oriental languages, the second,

that of all Christian knights there should be made a certain order, which should strive continually for the conquest of the Holy Land.[2]

With the third we shall be concerned in a later section.

Was the change of front occasioned by the ill-success of his missionary labours? Though he wrote much, he visited North Africa only three times, and in each case his stay was a brief one. It is not surprising that his method at Bugia brought him to prison. For he stood in the market-place and cried: 'The law of the Christians is holy and true, and the sect of the Moslems is false and wrong, and this I am prepared to prove.'[3] He did not doubt that he himself was in possession of the truth and that those to

---

[1] E. Allison Peers, *Ramon Lull*, London: S.P.C.K., 1929, pp. 30 f.
[2] Ibid. p. 351.   [3] Ibid. p. 325.

whom he went were wilfully in error. He had complete confidence in his ability to demonstrate the truth of the Trinity and the Incarnation. Did he not actually invent a sort of

logical machine, in which the subjects and predicates of theological propositions were arranged in circles, squares, triangles, and other geometrical figures, so that by moving a lever, turning a crank, or causing a wheel to revolve, the propositions would arrange themselves in affirmation or negation, and thus prove themselves to be true?[1]

Apparently, therefore, Lull accepted the current view that Christianity and Islam were related simply as truth and error. But this was not quite the case. As a student of Islam, he could not but be aware that it had much in common with his own faith. So, in the *Book of the Gentile*, he introduces us to a Saracen who is called upon to state what he believes. Before speaking, he performs the prescribed lustrations, of which a detailed account is given, recites the opening sura of the Koran, and then gives a statement of his creed that shows how accurate was Lull's information.

In the main body of the book, three sages, a Jew, a Christian, and a Saracen are about to begin a discourse that has the unity of religion as its aim, when they are accosted by a heathen philosopher. He tells them that he sees death approaching and fears it may be the end. Can they not convince him of God and the resurrection? Since the three religions are united on these points, they are able to satisfy him. But when he asks why so little is done for those who share his ignorance, he learns how deeply his new acquaintances are divided. Each is convinced that his own religion is the one true faith and that eternal torment awaits those who profess one of the others. He begs therefore that each will state his case, so that he may choose between them. They speak in order of age, the Jew first, the Christian next, the Saracen last. So fairly is Islam represented that there is even a warning against supposing that its Paradise is a place of sensual delights merely. The philosopher appears to incline towards the

[1] *Catholic Encyclopaedia*, xii. 670.

Christian position, but he leaves without committing himself. The sages are impressed with the Gentile's concern for truth and vow to seek it as earnestly, by friendly discussion among themselves. What is remarkable is the objectivity of the whole treatment. Was Lull so confident of the Christian case that he could afford to be scrupulously fair to Judaism and Islam? Or was he merely reproducing the method of a medieval disputation? One explanation is clearly ruled out. His attitude was not one of indifference.

I have spoken of the effect on Lull of his study of Islam. Perhaps even more important was the effect of contact with Islam in the person of its followers. Like some in our own day, he contrasted the fervour of Moslem piety with the lukewarmness of so many Christians. Thus, *The Book of the Lover and the Beloved*, an appendix to the allegorical novel *Blanquerna* but a spiritual classic in its own right, is introduced with a reference to the Sufis who 'have words of love and brief examples which give to men great devotion'. At a later point in the book he writes:

> The Lover reproached Christian people, because in their letters they put not first the name of his Beloved, Jesus Christ, to do him the same honour that the Saracens do Mahomet, who was a knave and no true man, when they honour him by naming him in their letters first of all.[1]

Nor was Lull content merely to admire this aspect of Islam. He paid it the compliment of imitation. He composed *The Hundred Names of God* as a devotional collection to be used in churches, thus exceeding by one the divine attributes on which the devout Moslem is wont to meditate.

c. THE KORAN REFUTED

The career of Lull, as we have seen, shows how the condemnation of Islam as a false religion could be maintained even while it

[1] Peers, op. cit. p. 434.

was in fact qualified by the recognition, in the first place, of certain elements of truth within it, and, in the second, of a genuine spirituality in the life it inspired. As a further illustration of this I propose to take another of these thirteenth-century missionaries, the Dominican Ricoldo da Monte di Croce.[1] Ricoldo was the first European to give a precise account of conditions in Baghdad, the first also to derive his knowledge of Islam from Oriental sources and not merely from Moorish or Syrian. Setting out in 1288 on a pilgrimage to the Holy Land, he pushed on to Baghdad, where he enrolled as a student and was granted every facility for study. It is possible that he made a fresh translation of the Koran, but if so, it is lost to us. He left behind him two books, *Liber Peregrinacionis*,[2] an account of his travels and his first-hand contacts with Islam, and *Confutatio Alcorani*,[3] a systematic attempt to come to grips with its teaching. The latter received the compliment of a translation into German by Luther.[4]

In the *Confutatio Alcorani* Ricoldo repeats the usual slanders against the Prophet. He depicts Mohammed as a robber chieftain, as unscrupulous as he was cowardly and unsuccessful. He fixes on epilepsy as an important factor in his claim to inspiration. His appearance as a prophet was the work of Satan, incensed by Heraclius's recovery of the Cross from the Persians.[5] The choice of an agent was determined by Mohammed's evil qualities. No

[1] I follow the *Catholic Encyclopaedia* for the spelling of his name.

[2] Published in J. C. M. Laurent, *Peregrinationes Medii Aevi Quattuor*, 1873. See on this Ugo Monnerert de Villard, *Il Libro della Peregrinazione nella Parti d'Oriente de Fratre Ricoldo da Montecroce*, 1948.

[3] I have not been able to find a copy of this book that is not the translation of a translation. The Byzantine theologian Demetrius Cydonius rendered it into Greek when the Eastern Empire was menaced by Islam, and in 1506 this was translated back into Latin by the Italian Bartolomeo of Monte Arduo.

[4] Made in 1542 from Bartolomeo's Latin. Under the title *Verlegung Alcorans Bruder Richardi* it appears in vol. liii of the Weimar edition. The Latin text used by Luther is reproduced there, and footnotes indicate where it departs from the original. See Sweetman, *Islam and Christian Theology*, London: Lutterworth Press, 1945-48, ii/1. 116.

[5] Which, in fact, fell towards the close of the Prophet's life!

doubt, the devil would have preferred someone better, as more fitted to deceive. But the divine wisdom would not permit this, wanting it to be obvious to all what was taking place and how worthless the new religion was! Ricoldo can even say that Mohammed allowed his followers to indulge in unnatural vice. At one point he declares that 'what the Alcoran and the whole sect of Saracens have in mind is just this, that supreme blessedness lies in lust and gluttony'.[1] It is not surprising, therefore, that he recommended polemics rather than understanding to the would-be missionaries for whom the book was written. It is easier and therefore wiser to work by exposing the folly of Islam than by demonstrating the truth of the Gospel.

As a traveller in the Near East, however, Ricoldo had not failed to be impressed by the part that religion played in the life of the ordinary man, and the *Liber Peregrinacionis*, being written for the general public, presents a much more favourable view. He ascribes to Moslems numerous 'works of perfection', such as enthusiasm for study, devotion in prayer, charity towards the poor, reverence for the name of God, dignity in bearing, courtesy towards strangers, concord and love among themselves. He is struck by the number of students in Baghdad and the public provision for their maintenance. He notes how unfailingly his companions in travel observed the hours of prayer. The songs of the Saracens are hymns of praise and their conversation is marred neither by slander nor by gossip. The moral of it all is clear. If these lost souls will do so much for their 'law of death', why do we do so little for our 'law of life'?

For even after these admissions Ricoldo sees the issue as one of truth versus error. The Saracen law, we are told in the concluding sections, is lax, obscure, confused, and irrational. And he concludes with the pious hope that all who believe in so preposterous a religion will end in the flames of hell!

[1] Luther, op. cit. liii. 317.

d. AVERROES AND AQUINAS

I spoke earlier of the three-point programme prepared by Lull for the Council of Vienne. The time has now come to deal with the second of these points, which was

> that in opposition to the opinion of Averroes, who in many things has endeavoured to oppose the Catholic faith, men of learning should compose works refuting these errors aforementioned and all those that hold the same opinion.[1]

But if to Lull Averroes (Ibn Raschid) was an enemy to be opposed, he none the less represented an opportunity to be seized. The time was ripe for a mission to the Moslem world precisely because its religion was being undermined from within by the philosophers. Modern study of Averroes tends to acquit him of some of the major innovations of thought for which he has long been held responsible. Thus he did not, it would seem, teach the dangerous doctrine of a 'double truth', that what is true in theology may be false in philosophy, and vice versa. But he did recognize two formulations of truth, a supernatural revelation in the Koran and a natural theology in Aristotle, the former for the masses and the latter for the few who could appreciate it.[2]

There was a curious ambivalence in the attitude of thirteenth century Christendom to him. He was at once revered as an interpreter of Aristotle and detested as a source of pestilential heresies. Histories of philosophy tell of the acute controversies that followed on the publication of his writings in a Latin translation, and of the episcopal and Papal decisions that led to their condemnation. By the third quarter of the century, indeed, Averroes had become a symbol, a banner to which the freethinkers of the time rallied. And there were many such.

One item in what may be called the Averroes-legend is that which sent his sons to Sicily, to find a place at the court of Frederick II. This prince made no secret of his preference for

---

[1] Peers, op. cit. p. 351.   [2] *The Legacy of Islam*, pp. 275 ff.

Saracens, encouraged Arabic studies, and surrounded himself with sceptics and unbelievers. It was in such a circle that men began to speak of Christianity as one of three rival religions and to compare it unfavourably with Judaism and Islam. Rumour even told of a book *De Tribus Impostoribus* in which Moses, Jesus, and Mohammed in turn were held up to ridicule. No one, to be sure, had actually seen the book, but there were those who, so they affirmed, had met those who had seen it. No one doubted its existence or its blasphemous character. Who then was the author? Was it perhaps Averroes himself?

Thus, as Renan puts it, the thirteenth century conceived the idea of *a comparison between religions*. A few advanced thinkers could no longer class Christianity as the true faith and the rest as false. Some went on to hint that perhaps all were false. If so, then it might well be that Christianity, precisely because it claims to be alone true, is inferior to the others, which at least allow a relative value to their rivals. And Islam and Judaism, it was whispered, shared one outstanding advantage. Neither had a Pope!

Averroes, so the legend ran, had put this brutally: Christianity is impossible, Judaism is for children, and Islam is for pigs.[1] Another version had it that he professed each religion in turn and ended without any. He was a mad dog, barking incessantly against Christ and the Christian faith.[2] In this Averroes-legend Thomas Aquinas figures as the knight of faith, the St George who slays the philosopher-dragon.[3] We are told on what seems to be good authority that his *Summa Contra Gentiles* was written at the request of Ramon Pennyafort as a textbook of apologetics and missionary theology for use within the Dominican order. But allusions to Islam are few and far between and there are no indications that Aquinas took the trouble to acquit himself with its doctrines, except at hearsay. The passage in which he gives his estimate of Mohammed is too long to quote here and it has nothing of value to offer.[4] We are told that he

[1] Renan, *Averroes et l'Averroisme*, 1866, p. 297.
[2] Ibid. p. 299.　　　　[3] Ibid. pp. 301 ff. for this theme in Italian art.
[4] Op. cit. Dominican trans., i. 13.

enticed peoples with the promise of carnal pleasures, to the desires of which the concupiscence of the flesh instigates. He also delivered commandments in keeping with his promises, by giving the reins to carnal pleasure, wherein it is easy for carnal men to obey: and the lessons of truth which he inculcated were only such as can be easily known to any man of average wisdom by his natural powers.

As Chenu points out, the traditional view of the origin of the *Contra Gentiles*, if accepted *simpliciter*, raises more problems than it solves. We must therefore suppose that, whatever the audience Aquinas was instructed to address, the one he actually had in mind was that of the University of Paris. 'He has in view and seeks to refute the theses of the Averroism then current in Paris.'[1]

Yet modern scholarship, if it does not see Averroes as the dragon, is equally reluctant to cast Aquinas for the role of St George. We are told, for example, that 'coincidences between the theology of St Thomas and Averroes are extremely numerous' and that there must indeed be 'something firmer than coincidence' here. One is left wondering how this is to be reconciled with the assertion, made in the same quarters, that the Latin translations of Averroes sadly misrepresented him. But, whatever the explanation, the fact that we must recognize 'the presence of doctrines of Islam in the very citadel of Western Christianity, the Summa of Aquinas', is germane to our study. It is one more piece of evidence that the simple judgment truth versus error cannot in fact be maintained.[2]

e. AMONG THE MONGOLS

One of the most enterprising missionaries of the period was the Franciscan, William Rubruck, who entered the Mongol Empire and spent some time at the court of the Great Khan. He had been preceded in 1245 by John of Piano Carpini, sent by Pope Innocent IV thither to ward off the menace to Western Europe now that

---

[1] *Introduction à l'étude de Saint Thomas d'Aquin*, 1950, p. 250.
[2] *The Legacy of Islam*, pp. 279, 281.

Russia had been overrun and annexed; an embassy had also been sent by St Louis of France. These missions had been political in character, while William's was purely religious.

He came to a people who were among the great powers of their day; he expected too, that they would be prepared to listen to his message. For Christianity in its Nestorian form had long been established in Central Asia. Indeed adherents of it were to be found at the court and at times even in the royal family. In February 1258 a Mongol army sacked Baghdad and put an end to the Abbasid caliphate; two years later, a second army, led by a Christian general and allied with two Christian kings, captured Aleppo and Damascus. Brother William was among the Mongols from 1253 to 1255 so that he could scarcely have arrived at a more favourable moment.

Mango Khan, to whose court he came, was an idolater, but there was Moslems as well as Christians among his entourage. The Buddhists whom he also met were lamas such as are to be found in Tibet to this day. Through the indigenous Bon religion [1] that preceded it, Lamaism had absorbed elements from various sources, including Manichaeism, and William makes express mention of this. The 'idolatrous priests', as he calls them, shaved their heads, took a vow of chastity, and lived a communal life. They recited in their temples what were obviously Buddhist scriptures, and used rosaries, repeating as they told their beads the sacred formula *Om mani padi hum* ('Greeting to the jewel in the lotus'), which is clearly discernible in William's *On man baccam*. He took this to be a prayer, and we are not surprised to find that in a conversation conducted through an interpreter he reached strange results. He understood them at one point to say that they believed in one God who is spirit and at another to jeer at him

---

[1] 'Essentially a shamanist, devil-charming, necromantic cult with devil-dancing, allied to the Taoism of China.' ERE, xii. 333. 'The struggle between the two demiurges of good and evil is fundamental to the Bon conception of the universe. Their theology is thus definitely derived from Iranian and Manichaean sources.' Fosco Mariani, *Secret Tibet*, London: Hutchinson & Co., 1952, p. 166.

when he in turn spoke of God and the soul. This was not the last occasion on which Buddhist and Christian found it difficult to understand each other, because the language they employed was pre-empted for the expression of Buddhist ideas. Not to mention the additional complication introduced by an interpreter who was 'tired and unable to express the words'.

What must surely have been the first inter-religious conference in history, took place at Pentecost of 1254, and a panel of three judges, one from each religion, was appointed by the Khan to preside over the debate. The Nestorians asked William to represent the Christian cause, and he discussed with the lamas the unity and omnipotence of God and his relation to evil. When he declared that 'all things that are, are good', their Manichaeism was roused in protest. They 'were astonished at this saying and put it down in writing as something untrue and impossible'.[1] When they were forced to admit that, on their premises, there could be no omnipotent God, the Moslems joined in the laughter of the Christians. At this point the Nestorians intervened and proposed to argue with the Moslems, but the latter declined, actually assuring the Christians that 'in all their prayers they beseech God to grant that they may die a Christian death'. One suspects that this was the interpreter's way of cutting the discussion short.

Those who convene similar gatherings today might care to know how this one concluded.

When this was finished, the Nestorians and Saracens alike sang loudly while the *tuins* kept silence, and afterwards they all drank their fill.[2]

On his return William sent a report of his travels to St Louis and, after staying some time at Acre, made his way to Paris, where he met Roger Bacon, who was not a little intrigued to hear of this conference. In his *Opus Maius* Bacon tells of his

[1] *The Mongol Mission*, ed. Christopher Dawson, London: Sheed & Ward, 1955, p. 193. [2] Ibid. p. 194.

meeting with the intrepid Franciscan. What William related of his travels helped him in his classification of religions under six heads: (1) Pagans, i.e. worshippers of natural phenomena; (2) Idolators, worshippers of manufactured images; (3) Tartars, who cultivated philosophy and magic arts; (4) Saracens; (5) Jews; (6) Christians. Pagans and idolaters are obviously in error, and Bacon understands the Tartars to have admitted defeat at the conference. What he has to say of the Jews does not concern us, and he has little to add to what his predecessors urged against Islam. While various Christian doctrines were adumbrated by the philosophers, this is not the case with Islam, whose philosophers are openly critical of their religion. Indeed he makes them give it only another generation to live. The points at which Christianity is found superior are miracles, fulfilment of prophecy, and sexual restraint by virginity and in marriage as opposed to the license permitted and practised by Mohammed. In addition, the virgin birth of Jesus, admitted by the Koran, ranks him higher than Mohammed.[1]

[1] *Opus Maius*, ed. J. H. Bridges, 1897, ii. 367 ff.

II

A Vision of Unity

a. NICOLAS OF CUSA

The thirteenth century ended with the triumph of Islam and the extinction of the tiny Christian kingdoms of Palestine. Before the following century was halfway through, a Moslem army had set foot on European soil in the East, and that at the invitation of a Christian. A few years later, an Ottoman garrison at Gallipoli was evidence enough that the Byzantine Empire, long since shorn of its Asiatic provinces, was now threatened in its very capital. The one hope of deliverance lay in an appeal to Western Christendom. To effect this, there must first be a reconciliation with the Roman Church. The Council of Basel took the initiative and invited the Emperor, John Paleologus, to come in person to conduct negotiations. An escort was sent to Constantinople in 1437 and one of its members was Nicolas of Cusa. This expedition brought him into indirect contact with Islam.

His reaction to it marks a distinct advance upon that of his predecessors. He endeavoured to refute it, of course, and he could be as harsh in his judgments on the Prophet as anyone before him. But the title he gave to his polemic work, *Cribratio Alcorani*, is indicative of a new spirit. He wants to sift the book, to separate the true in it from the false. Indeed, he actually extended the range of his interest so far as to include Judaism and the pagan cults, along with Islam, as so many types of religion that could in some sense be set alongside Christianity. He first in Christendom envisaged the possibility of mutual understanding on the part of the various faiths, and in *De Pace Fidei* he argued for this. If we ask how such an outlook, impossible in others, was actual in Nicolas, the answer is that a passion for unity, both theoretical and practical, was one of his characteristics. Thus, he was one of the envoys appointed at Basel to negotiate with the Hussite leaders, and the agreement of 1433 was largely his work.

But it is the dating of the amazingly irenical *De Pace Fidei* that is so remarkable. It was written in the very year in which Constantinople fell to Islam (May 29, 1453). The alternative to crusades was not now missions, it was the harmony of religions. To be sure, Constantinople was not yet abandoned as lost, and there was talk in the West of an expedition to recover it. Nicolas made his contribution to the proposed counter-attack with the book *Cribratio Alcorani*, written probably in 1461 or late in 1460.[1] It is dedicated to Pius II, for his use in the refutation and condemnation of Moslem errors. In our discussion of the two books, it will be more convenient to begin with the one that was published later.

b. MOHAMMED AS WITNESS TO CHRIST

Anything like a systematic account of the contents of the *Cribratio* would need to be preceded by an outline of Nicolas's philosophy, since this is operative throughout. I shall only touch on this where it proves absolutely necessary; my concern is with the attempt to present Mohammed as a witness to Christ, since this is a new approach to the Koran. Not that Nicolas does not parade the old slanders and indulge in the old polemic. He is never sure whether to execrate Mohammed as the enemy of Christ or to acclaim him as a witness to him. Our concern is solely with the second presentation.

Nicolas states at the outset what his purpose is. He proposes to sift the Koran and to show that it contains much that would confirm the Gospel, did this need confirmation; also that where it departs from the Gospel it does so as a result of Mohammed's

---

[1] *Sichtung des Alcorans*, ed. Paul Naumann, 1948, p. 13.

ignorance and therefore of his evil intent.[1] He actually hazards the suggestion that, in spite of Nestorian and Jewish influence, Mohammed himself revered Christ as Son of God and believed in his death for the salvation of mankind. But he thought it inexpedient to express himself clearly. Perhaps he adopted a policy of accommodation as Jesus did in his parables, veiling the truth so that only those able to appreciate it would be in a position to receive it. Of one thing he is sure, and that is that such truth as the Koran possesses has been borrowed from the Gospel.

If therefore any beauty, truth, and light are found in the Koran, it must be that this is a ray from that Gospel which is the fulness of light. And he who reads first the Gospel and then the Koran will see that this is so.[2]

In accordance with a tradition at least as early as John of Damascus, Mohammed is presented as a Christian heretic.[3] An expelled monk, Sergius by name, went to Mecca, where he preached his Nestorian version of Christianity to Jews and idolaters. Mohammed was converted by him and actually died a Christian. Before then, however, three crafty Jews had been at work upon him to turn him from the faith, and at his death, on which followed a general return to idolatry, they exploited his name for anti-Christian purposes. That is to say, they persuaded Mohammed's son-in-law Ali to come forward as a prophet and the successor of Mohammed, who now was made out to have been himself a prophet. Ali handed over to these Jews the writings his father-in-law had left behind him, and by a process of addition and subtraction they quite altered their character. They now became the documents of a new sect in which—contrary to Mohammed's own attitude—Jews were equally esteemed with

---

[1] *Sichtung des Alcorans*, ed. Paul Naumann, 1948, p. 83: *De Nicolai de Cusa Cardinalis Opera*, Basel, 1565, p. 881. Some chapters of the *Cribratio* are translated into French by Maurice de Gandillac in *Oeuvres Choisis de Nicolas de Cusa*. See Sweetman, op cit. ii/1. 159 f.

[2] Ibid. p. 105; ibid. p. 888.

[3] Migne: *Patrologia Graeca*, cxiv. 678 ff.

Christians. On this view, what is true in the Koran is of Christian origin, though not orthodox, while what is false is the perverse work of Jewish intriguers.

There is even evidence, Nicolas thinks, that Mohammed knew the full truth about Christ though he did not proclaim it openly. Here the Latin translation he uses has led him astray. Where in the original Jesus is described as 'illustrious in this world and the next' (iii. 40), the Latin has *facies omnium gentium*, prototype of all peoples. Naturally enough, Nicolas cites this passage again and again. Further, the Koran speaks of Christ as the Word of God but will not allow that God has a Son. But the difference here, Nicolas suggests, may be one of language only. God does not 'have' a Son, as he does not 'have' anything whatsoever. With him, having and being are one, yet we may not say that the Father 'is' the Son. Perhaps Mohammed shrank from speaking of Christ as Son because this would be misunderstood by idolaters, who would infer either a plurality of gods or a physical sonship rather than an intellectual one.

The same subtlety enables Nicolas to find an affirmation of the death and resurrection of Christ even in those passages that explicitly deny these. What could be made of the plain assertion in the Koran that Jesus did not die, but that another was crucified in his place? The least satisfactory expedient is to say that the Koran does not deny that Jesus was crucified, but only that the Jews crucified him. As to be sure they did not. The Romans did! Another suggestion is that Mohammed thought death out of place with such an one as Christ. He could not grasp the mystery of a death by which a cross became a throne. As for the resurrection—there the argument becomes even more involved and even less convincing.

We are left wondering why Nicolas is at such pains to demonstrate that the Koran does not mean what it says. This is one of those points at which the polemic tendency yields to the irenic. The final conclusion of the book is that Mohammed knew who Jesus was and what happened to him, but knew also that the ignorant and uncultured Arabs of his day would not listen to such a message. He could not have convinced them of Christ's death and resurrection without acknowledging his divinity, and this, so far as he could see, was not consistent with the unity of God. He therefore simplified his preaching till it was well within their understanding, presenting Christ for the time being as the greatest of prophets and of men.

Therefore Mohammed concealed from them the mysteries of the Gospel, to the intent that they should one day be revealed to the wise, just as the Gospel at first remained obscure to many and was not understood, but only gradually became more and more manifest.[1]

Almost all this reasoning is forced and much of it is based on crass misunderstanding of the text. But all honour is due to one who, in spite of the misleading sources on which he drew, in spite also of the mortal danger in which Christendom stood from Islam, could not dismiss it out of hand as a false religion. The light of Christ shines in it too.

c. A VISION OF UNITY

We now come to *De Pace Fidei*, in which Nicolas actually envisages the possibility of a universal religion on which Jews, Christians and Moslems will agree. The immediate occasion for its composition was the capture of Constantinople in 1453 and the atrocities by which this was accompanied. Shocked by the strife and cruelty that issued from religious differences, Nicolas prayed that they might somehow be led to agree and so restore peace to mankind. In a vision, he saw the Lord of all surrounded by his heavenly court. The most eminent of the Archangels took up his petition. There is but one God after whom all men seek, since all seek the good and the true: let God reveal Himself and convince men that 'under the diversity of religious practices there is but one religion'. Here we have the key to the whole book. Nicolas proposes to apply to the non-Christian religions the

[1] *Sichtung*, pp. 202 f.: *Opera*, p. 904.

principle that worked in the case of the Greeks and the Hussites. Nations develop their own customs and in course of time become so attached to these that nothing will induce them to abandon them. And why should they? But why should they remain apart and hostile on that account? The unity of religion requires only agreement on essentials; on non-essentials let there by full toleration. An admirable formula, no doubt, but who decides what is essential and what is not?

In the vision the Word seconds the archangel's petition and God bids the angels who have oversight of the nations summon an assembly of their wise men to reduce the variety of religions to the one true faith.

He is convinced that, as religion is natural to all men, so the basic ideas of Christianity are accepted implicitly by all. The wise may be persuaded of this by reasoning, while the prejudices of the multitude can be respected where they do not militate against this universal faith. The discussion takes the form of a series of questions addressed to the Word by the spokesmen of various nations, and answered through the medium, first of Peter then of Paul. The Greek and the Italian represent philosophy, and they are easily brought to acknowledge that Wisdom is one and that it is God, 'the one simple, eternal God, the source of all'.[1] The Arabian, who stands for Islam in its philosophical rather than its religious aspects, agrees, but asks what then is to be done with polytheists? The reply is that those who worship many gods may yet seek in them all the one Godhead. Provided they will recognize him and worship him in the full sense, there is no reason why they should not venerate holy men. So with idols. They can be permitted where they aid men to worship the one true God, but not where they draw them away from him.

The crux of the whole discussion is, of course, the Trinity and the Incarnation. These for Nicolas are among the essentials, Christian dogmas that must enter into any universal religion.

---

[1] *Uber den Frieden im Glauben*, ed. Ludwig Moehler, 1943, p. 93; *De Pace Fidei*, ed. Klibansky and Bascovy, 1956. See Gandillac, op. cit. also Sweetman, op. cit. ii/1. 170 ff.

He tries to show that they are not inconsistent with the unity of God; indeed, that they follow logically from it. Here he has recourse to the philosophy expounded in all his writings.[1] On the one hand, by the principles of negative theology, God is absolute and inexpressible.

As infinite he is neither threefold nor one nor yet any of the attributes that can be ascribed to him. For the names that are applied to God are taken from the creatures, since in Himself he is inexpressible and exalted above all that can be named or spoken of.[2]

On the other hand, positive theology speaks of him, not as he is in himself, but as he is in relation to the world. That world is characterized by multiplicity, inequality, and division. God is prior to these as eternal unity, equality and connection, and in him these three are one. So those who grant the unity confess the Trinity implicitly in so doing. A similar argument is developed in the case of the Incarnation.

If the universal religion is to have so much Christian dogma, will it have any Christian rites? Certainly, says our cardinal. Yet these are of much less importance in his eyes. For faith and love alone are essential and alone are necessary to salvation. On circumcision, it might seem that the best course would be for the Christians to submit to this in return for the acceptance of so much of their dogma by Jews and Moslems. This, however, is scarcely practicable, so it is to be hoped that the majority will fall in with the minority on this point. Non-Christians are to accept the Eucharist, but a rational account of transubstantiation is given so as to relieve it of any charge of materialism. The method of its administration is one of those points on which liberty of opinion can safely be conceded.

How shall we judge of this scheme? It is possible to brand it as hopelessly conservative. In the sphere of dogma, peace is made

[1] See especially *Of Learned Ignorance*, trans. Germain Heron, London: Routledge & Kegan Paul, 1954.

[2] *Frieden*, p. 107; *De Pace*, p. 20.

on one condition—that other religions surrender to Christianity. Baptism and the Mass, ordination and marriage are to be accepted by all, though in return there need be no uniformity on such matters as fasting and forms of prayer. Let the different nations thereby provoke each other to greater zeal. On the other hand, there are some remarkably liberal features. The disquisition on justification by faith, while hardly Protestant in tone, shows a new interest in Paul. And what shall we think of a cardinal who says not so much as a word on the authority of the Church or submission to the Pope? We may suspect that he was prepared to go farther in his toleration of a diversity of rites than most of those in his position would have done. The humanism of the Renaissance was at work in him.

The cynic might say that this solution of the problem is naïve in the extreme. Peace between the religions is possible if only all will accept—the philosophy of Nicolas of Cusa. But what else could he have said? What have we to urge upon our fellows except what we believe to be true? Neither to the writer nor to the reader of this book is any other course open.

III

The Impact of China

a. THE REFORMATION

To the Renaissance and the Reformation the non-Christian
world was still that of Nicolas of Cusa, the world of Judaism,
Islam, and paganism. Luther knew the non-Christian only as
either the Turk, or the Jew, and when he translated Ricoldo's
Confutatio into German, he did it partly as an encouragement of
Christians perplexed by the advance of Islam and partly as a
polemic against the Pope, a worse Antichrist even than Mohammed. The discovery of America did not alter the position substantially; it merely enlarged the area occupied by paganism and
deprived of the Gospel. When the Reformers therefore discussed
the salvation of the heathen, they did so in terms of classical and
biblical precedents. Zwingli, for example, did not doubt that
there would be a place in heaven for Hercules and Theseus as well
as Socrates.

In short, there has not lived a single good man, there has not been a
single pious heart or believing soul from the beginning of the world
to the end, which you will not see there in the presence of God.

All that he has to say of Islam is casual, ill-informed, and mere
repetition of the prejudices we have already met with.[1]
There were those, to be sure, who were prepared to go even
farther than Zwingli, and among these the most notable is
Sebastian Franck. His 'spiritualism', his individual piety and his

[1] *Zwingli and Bullinger* (Library of Christian Classics), 1953, p. 276.

detachment from all the churches betray the influence of the mediaeval mystics and the humanists, Erasmus among them. He represented that 'universal religion of theism or panentheism' in which Dilthey sees 'the highest and freest element in European culture' at that time.[1] One of his warmest admirers says of him that he created an amalgam and not a synthesis, a mosaic arranged around certain leading ideas.[2] One of these ideas is that of the opposition between the inward and the outward. All religions are relative, because they are so many exteriorizations of the spirit, so many representations of God under a historically conditioned form. The one true religion is the worship of God in spirit and in truth. The actual religions, Christianity among them, are therefore true in so far as they participate in this, false in so far as they depart from it, substituting externals for the inward disposition. Since God is pure goodness, his revelation is for all men at all times; he discloses himself to them inwardly by reason and conscience. All who obey the inward monitor are therefore children of God and acknowledged as such by him. God is no respecter of persons, and the pious heathen is on the same level as the Christian in his sight. Franck mentions Socrates and Plato, Hermes Trismegistus and the Sibyl among those who knew God by the natural light.

At the same time, he personally is a Christian and he is prepared to maintain that salvation is by Christ alone. How are the two positions to be reconciled? He falls back on the Logos-doctrine of the Alexandrian Fathers and with its help he equates Christ with the Inner Light, with reason and conscience as they are present in every man. 'All salvation is mediated through Christ, but it is not the historical Christ who bestows it, it is the ideal Christ.'[3] Yet the historical Christ is of decisive importance;

---

[1] *Gesammelte Werke*, ii. 81.   [2] A. Koyré, *Sebastien Franck*, 1932, pp. 8 f.
[3] A. Hegler, *Geist und Schrift bei Sebastian Franck*, 1892, p. 199. So for Dirk Coornheert the 'Indwelling Christ reaches out far beyond the borders of Christendom, since, apart from the Scriptures, the Logos has brought new light and life to many souls in the non-Christian world'. Troeltsch, *The Social Teaching of the Christian Churches*, London: Allen & Unwin, 1931, ii. 764.

he bears witness to, makes manifest, the eternal truth that is written on the heart of man as such. His true church is therefore invisible and spiritual, to be found among Christians and heathen alike. There are thoughts here with which we shall be concerned in the sequel.

Unfortunately, there were limits to the charity of so great a soul. Judaism he dismissed as a religion of external observances, its spirit long since dead. Of Mohammed he knew only the current slanders and he repeated them without examination. The prophet was a blind leader of the blind, propagating religion sword in hand. He won men by sensual delights and the indulgence of the passions. That the divine government of the world allowed such a man to appear and work so much harm could be explained in one way only; he was an instrument of God to punish apostate Christendom.[1]

The Reformation, then, was not open to the non-Christian world. The Counter-Reformation was, and its missionaries, recruited largely from the Society of Jesus, entered India, China and Japan. So doing they rediscovered the strange world that Marco Polo had visited. His report of what he found there had been dismissed as a traveller's tale; the accounts sent home by the Jesuits were taken seriously and became a factor of no slight importance in the intellectual life of Europe.

b. MISSIONS TO CHINA

This is not the place for more than a brief reference to the story of Jesuit missionary enterprise in China. There were two important phases in this. The first began with the arrival of Matteo Ricci at Goa in 1578. Five years later, he and a companion had established themselves in the neighbourhood of Canton. At first they dressed as Buddhist monks, but soon found that this carried with it no prestige. So, since their aim was to reach the upper class, they decided to adopt the dress of scholars. In their new role and with their knowledge of Western science they were able to enter into

---

[1] Arnold Reimann, *Sebastian Franck als Geschichtsphilosoph*, 1923, p. 72.

polite society and even to win converts. Ricci made his way to Pekin, where the present of a clock to the emperor secured him, if not permission to reside in the capital, at least toleration there. The mission was reinforced from Europe by men of outstanding ability, with such success that an imperial decree entrusted some of them with the reform of the calendar. John Adam Schall supervised the casting of cannon for the defence of Pekin against the Manchus, and his skill won such respect that the conquerors in turn took him into their service.

Not until the third decade of the seventeenth century did other orders establish themselves in China, notably the Dominicans and Franciscans. Meantime—and with this we come to the second phase—Louis XIV saw in a French mission to China an opportunity to enhance his prestige, and in the second half of the century the *Société des Missions Étrangères* came into being. Its agents worked at first in Siam and Indo-China, but later extended their operations to China. In 1683 six French Jesuits, specially selected for their scientific knowledge, sailed for China under royal patronage. The emperor Kang H'si was one of the most enlightened of Chinese rulers, and in 1692 he issued the long-desired edict of toleration. Meanwhile, friction had developed between the various orders and nationalities with interests in the country.

From the beginning Ricci adopted the policy of 'accommodation'. He wanted to make the transition to Christianity as easy and as natural as possible, and also to defend himself against the charge of introducing a foreign religion. He took the view that the traditional ceremonies in honour of Confucius and the ancestors were civil and not religious in character, so that a Christian might legitimately take part in them, if the laws of the empire so required. There was also the question of the Chinese equivalent for 'God'. While normally using *T'ien Chu* (Lord of Heaven), Ricci was prepared to take from the classics the terms *Shang Ti* and Heaven. Not all the Jesuits agreed with him, but the really bitter opposition came from the Dominicans. The controversy was carried on in Europe as well as China, and while Rome was considering what decision to reach, the emperor identified himself with the Jesuits. When therefore the Pope in 1704 finally gave judgment against them, the emperor was incensed at what he considered interference in a domestic concern. Meanwhile, in Europe itself powerful forces were at work against the order, and submission became inevitable. But this brought on it the imperial displeasure, persecution broke out again, and an enterprise once so promising was brought to a standstill. Long before that happened, however, the Jesuits had translated into Latin some of the Chinese classics and given to Europe their impressions of a civilization that compared favourably with its own. In addition, some of them had revisited their own countries and excited intense interest by their reports. For they offered a momentous, perhaps even a decisive, contribution to the debate in which Europe was engaged.

Sick of rival creeds and devasting wars of religion, men everywhere were turning to 'natural religion' as the one possible basis of agreement. Here was a religion for all sensible men, a welcome end to fanaticism of every kind. One of the best and most influential statements of this position was Lord Herbert of Cherbury's *De Veritate*. According to him, man shares with the animal a natural instinct for self-preservation, though in him it assumes a higher form, becoming spiritual and no longer merely biological. It therefore equips him with certain 'common notions'. These are axiomatic, basic to our thinking. They are like Kant's categories inasmuch as they are presupposed in all experience, and indeed constitutive of it. These common notions are five in number. They are (*a*) the existence and attributes of God, (*b*) his claim to worship, (*c*) the connection between virtue and piety, (*d*) repentance for wrong-doing, and (*e*) rewards and punishments after death. And

the only Catholic and uniform Church is the doctrine of Common Notions which comprehends all places and all men. This Church alone reveals Divine Universal Providence, or the wisdom of Nature. And it is only through this Church that salvation is possible.[1]

[1] Lord Herbert of Cherbury, *De Veritate*, trans. Carré, 1937, p. 303.

Herbert did not deny revelation, but he was suspicious of it. He commends the attitude of the 'cautious layman', who demands cogent proofs before he will credit the priests farther than these common notions allow. Such indeed was the attitude of intelligent men in the ancient world. Their real religion was that set out above: all else they either dismissed as absurd or at best tolerated with a smile.

In the course of the debate certain crucial questions emerged. Is belief in God universal or are there peoples to whom this is unknown? Is such belief necessary to personal morality and social order or is atheism compatible therewith? What is the relation, for those who allow revelation, between this and natural religion? As long as the discussion was purely theoretical it was likely to remain inconclusive. But the news from China suggested that there was an alternative. For had not that country staged an immense and protracted experiment that would provide a definitive answer to precisely these questions?

c. JESUIT WITNESS

What was the judgment of these Jesuit missionaries on the religion they found in China? I shall call in evidence four witnesses. They represent the majority opinion, though there were dissenters within the order.

(i) The first is Matteo Ricci himself. He distinguished between the original texts of the classics and the interpretation put upon them by the dominant Sung philosophy. As to the religious implications of this philosophy let a contemporary Chinese scholar speak:

> This attempt to humanise the K'ung (Confucian) doctrine had also the indirect effect of ultimately doing away with the ancient Sinitic conception of heaven as a personalized god. . . . And now, with the mysteries of the creation satisfactorily explained in terms of metaphysics, it is obvious that there would be no further use for an almighty god as the ruling deity of men.[1]

[1] Liu Wu-chi, *A Short History of Confucian Philosophy*, London: Penguin Books, 1955, p. 164.

It was precisely this 'ancient Sinitic conception of heaven as a personalized god' that gave the missionary his *point d'appui* in approaching the scholar class. The Shang Ti, the Heaven, and the Lord of heaven were for him so many names for the one great and good God, maker and ruler of all things. In other words, he found in Confucius the natural theology, the *preparatio evangelica*, of China as his theological training had given him this for the West in Aristotle.

Hence his most important work in Chinese was the catechism *The True Doctrine of God*, which ran through five editions during his lifetime. We are told that 'it led countless numbers to Christianity, and aroused esteem for our religion in those readers whom it did not convert'.[1] The book, we are told,

consisted entirely of arguments from the natural light of reason, rather than such as are based upon the authority of Holy Scripture. In this way the road was levelled and made clear for the acceptance of the mysteries dependent upon faith and upon the knowledge of divine revelation. The book also contained citations serving its purpose and taken from the ancient Chinese writers; passages which were not merely ornamental, but served to promote the acceptance of this work by the enquiring readers of other Chinese books. It also provided a refutation of all the Chinese religious sects, excepting the one founded on the natural law, as developed by their Prince of Philosophers, Confucius, and adopted by the sect of the literati. Their particular philosophy as developed by the ancients, contains but little that is justly reprehensible. . . . The reply made by Doctor Paul, when he was asked, what he considered to be the basis of the Christian law, might be quoted here, as being very timely. He defined the whole subject in four syllables, or rather, in four words, when he said, Ciue, Po, Fu, Giu, meaning, It does away with idols and completes the law of the literati.[2]

(ii) Nicolas Trigault arrived in Macao in the year of Ricci's death (1610): by this time the mission had established itself so

[1] *Catholic Encyclopaedia*, xiii. 36.
[2] *China in the Sixteenth Century:* The Journals of Matthew Ricci, trans. Louis J. Gallagher, New York: Random House, 1942, p. 448.

securely that a few years later he was sent back to Europe to recruit new workers. On the voyage home he translated into Latin the Journals kept by his great predecessor, prefacing them with an account of China and its people from his own pen. Arrived in Rome, he presented the completed work to the Pope, and it was published in 1615 under the title *De Christiana expeditione apud Sinas ab Societate Jesu*. Translations soon followed into French, German, and Spanish. Like Ricci, Trigault distinguished sharply between the Buddhist bonzes and the literati. But he was struck by the similarity of the Pure Land sect of Buddhism to the Catholicism he had brought from Europe.

This philosophy seems not only to have borrowed from the West but to have actually caught a glimpse of light from the Christian Gospels . . . In some respects their profane rites resemble our own ecclesiastical ceremonies, as for instance their recitation in chant which hardly differs from our Gregorian.[1]

His final judgment is remarkable for its charity.

One can confidently hope that, in the mercy of God, many of the ancient Chinese found salvation in the natural law, assisted as they must have been by that special help which, as the theologians teach, is denied to no one who does what he can toward salvation, according to the light of his conscience. That they endeavoured to do this is readily determined from their history of more than four thousand years, which really is a record of good deeds done on behalf of their country and for the common good.[2]

(iii) The most important work for which the Jesuits were responsible was *Confucius Sinarum Philosophus*, published in Paris in 1687 with a dedication to Louis XIV. It contained a Life of Confucius, followed by translations of the Great Learning, the

[1] L. J. Gallagher, *The China That Was*, from the Latin of Nicolas Trigault, S.J., New York: Bruce Pub. Co., 1942, p. 164.

[2] Ibid. p. 154. On the position of Jesuit theologians in Europe see Louis Caperan, *Le problème de salut des infidèles*, 1934, i. 278 ff.

Doctrine of the Mean, and the Analects. Four scholars collaborated in it, Couplet, Herbtrich, Intorcetta, and Rougemont. Chronological tables traced the origin of the Chinese nation to the time of the Deluge. Basing on this, Louis Le Comte took a farther step in his *Nouveaux memoires sur l'état present de la Chine* (Paris, 1696). The appeal to natural law was not enough, the Chinese were declared to be repositories of revelation. As the immediate descendants of Noah, the founders of the Chinese empire carried with them almost intact the revelation of God at the beginning of the race. The third emperor built the most ancient temple in the world and sacrificed to the true God long before this was done in Israel. Only gradually did deterioration set in, and even then it was never total.

For more than two thousand years China preserved the knowledge of the true God and practised the purest maxims of morality while Europe and almost all the rest of the world were in error and corruption.[1]

The theological faculty at the Sorbonne thought otherwise. If the Chinese had got so far without revelation, what need was there for it. The Jesuit plea that there *had* been revelation did not receive the consideration it deserved. In 1700 a series of propositions extracted from Le Comte's work were censured and condemned as heretical. While the discussion continued, an opponent of the Jesuits put clearly what seemed to him at stake.

If all those who have lived according to reason, whether Jews or Gentiles, were truly and properly Christians and in a state of salvation, like those who had faith and to whom Jesus Christ was revealed, it becomes possible to save oneself by the capacities of nature, and faith in Jesus Christ as mediator is entirely unnecessary.[2]

(iv) It might well appear that this was as far as one could go towards meeting Confucianism halfway. But it was not. There

[1] G. Atkinson, *Les relations de voyages du XVIIe siècle*, p. 93.
[2] Ibid. p. 97, see also Caperan, op. cit. pp. 362 ff.

was a group of Jesuits known as the 'figurists' whose theories were so extreme that their superiors in Europe refused to give them to the public. Bouvet was among the most ardent of these. In a letter to Leibniz, dated from Pekin November 8, 1702, he went so far as to assert that

almost the whole system of the true religion is to be found in the classical books of the Chinese, and that the principal mysteries of the incarnation of the Word, the life and death of the Saviour, and the chief functions of his holy ministry are contained in the precious monuments of ancient China as it were in prophetic fashion.[1]

It was particularly the I-king or Book of Changes that Bouvet had in mind. Not that it was an inspired work on the same level as the Old Testament, but it preserved an original revelation that had been lost elsewhere or obscured beyond all recognition. The chronology with which the Chinese historians worked made it impossible to argue, as had once been done, that the wisdom of the Gentiles was borrowed from Moses. It must, in the case of China, go back to Noah if not indeed—as Bouvet suggested—to Enoch, who in turn drew on oral traditions coming down from Adam. What an argument with which to confute sceptics at home! What they challenged was shown to be part of the human heritage from the beginning of the race. And what an argument against heretics, too! For, writes Bouvet,

it will be seen that the prophets and holy teachers of the natural law must have had almost as much light on the principal mysteries of the law of Jesus Christ as the holy Fathers had, and that the Church the Son of God established on earth is truly catholic and universal for all periods of time as for all places on the earth.[2]

His superiors were not prepared to have the church as universal as that. The whole scheme was too much like a Christian version

[1] Leibniz, *Oeuvres* (Geneva, Fratres de Tournes), 1768, iv/1. 165.
[2] Virgile Pinot, *La Chine et la formation de l'esprit philosophique en France 1640-1740*, 1932, pp. 352 f.

of Lord Herbert of Cherbury, with dogmas reduced to 'common notions'. But there was no point in risking a heresy trial, as the order had enemies enough already. So these novel ideas got no farther than scholars like Leibniz who were in correspondence with individual missionaries.

d. BELIEVERS

We have followed the Jesuit reports on Confucianism, most of them remarkably favourable and some even extravagantly so. What was the reception accorded to them in Europe? Some believed and some doubted. For in Europe at the time there was much that disposed men to accept this story of a society superior to their own in morals and political science, with much to teach in the art of civilized living. Criticism of existing institutions sought support in travellers' tales of remote and simple peoples with none of Europe's vices because they were so much nearer to nature.

The Kindly Savage, the Wise Egyptian, the Mohammedan Arab, the Turkish, or Persian, Satirist—all these were highly diverting and most welcome to those who were looking for a new order of things. But still more popular than any of these was the Chinese Sage.[1]

Among the believers the chief place must go to Leibniz as a champion of natural religion who found an ally in China and the Jesuits. On a visit to Rome in 1689 he met one of the missionaries, Grimaldi by name, and gained from him first-hand knowledge of the country. On Grimaldi's return to China he corresponded with him. A letter written in December of the same year shows that he had read *Confucius Sinarum Philosophus*, and in the same month he writes suggesting that he put a notice on his door *Bureau d'adresse pour la Chine*, so busy is he collecting and disseminating information about the country.[2] In the preface

[1] Paul Hazard, *The European Mind* (1680-1715), 1935, p. 24.
[2] R. F. Merkel, *Leibniz und die Chinamission*, 1952, p. 17.

to *Novissima Sinica* he singles out for special mention as characteristic of Chinese society the stability of family life, based as it is on
respect for age, the public peace and social order everywhere
manifest, the mutual deference and courtesy that enter into daily
intercourse. Then follow the remarkable words:

The condition of affairs among ourselves seems to me to be such
that, in view of the inordinate lengths to which the corruption of
morals has advanced, I almost think it necessary that Chinese missionaries should be sent to us to teach us the aim and practice of natural
theology, as we send missionaries to them to instruct them in revealed
theology. For I believe that if a wise man were to be appointed judge—
not of the beauty of goddesses, but of the goodness of peoples—he
would award the golden apple to the Chinese—unless indeed we should
outdo them in nobility by conferring on them that which is, indeed, a
superhuman good—the divine gift of the Christian religion.[1]

Leibniz suggests that the West may have something to learn
from the East, but that the West has also something to give.

Even greater was the enthusiasm for China of Christian
Wolff. The furore provoked by his rectoral address *De Sinarum
Philosophia Practica* was such as to lead to his expulsion from the
University of Halle and the Prussian dominions. He borrows
from the Jesuits but differs from the majority of them on the
crucial point. That is to say, he is sure that the ancient Chinese had
no knowledge of God, whether natural or revealed. Longobardi,
who succeeded Ricci as head of the China mission, had taken this
view and was critized for it by Leibniz. Wolff prefers his finding
to Ricci's. In their achievements, as in their standards, the ancient
Chinese drew on their unaided natural resources. They have
therefore proved, for all to see, that human powers are sufficient to
enable us to choose good and refuse evil. The Chinese ethic is
purely rational, humanist, and utilitarian, with no appeal to
authority and no sanction in a life after death. The good is that
which ministers to the happiness and development of individual

[1] *Oeuvres*, iv/1. 82. The translation is from Reichwein, *China and Europe*,
1925, pp. 80 f.

and society alike. Yet, while it differs *toto caelo* from the Christian ethic as far as ground and motive are concerned, it does not differ appreciably in content. To harmonize the two systems, we have only to suppose that God forbids certain courses of action because he sees that they will promote the welfare of society and forbids others because they will injure it.[1]

There were even those who gave credence to the fantasies of the Figurists. The Chevalier Ramsey appeals to them in *Les Voyages de Cyrus* (1728). The appendix includes information from an authority on China, 'a gentleman of superior genius, who does not care to be mentioned till he has published a large work upon these matters'. The extracts from the Chinese classics that he sent to Ramsey and that are reproduced by him are obviously his allegorical interpretations rather than the original texts. The book itself is written to show that

the doctrines of the primitive perfection of nature, its fall, and its restoration by a divine Hero, are equally manifest in the Mythologies of the Greeks, Egyptians, Persians, Indians, and Chinese.[2]

This is the thesis of a primitive revelation that we have met already and shall meet again.

Last but not least among the supporters of the Jesuits in this matter I would cite Voltaire. He is sure that the ancient religion of China was the worship of one Supreme Being, without idolatry or superstition, and that this is still the creed of the scholar class. The accusation of idolatry brought against them is due to misunderstanding; gestures and actions implying no more than deep respect have been mistaken for worship. What idolatry obtains in China is due to Taoism and Buddhism and was always scorned by Confucians. He does not lose an opportunity to contrast the tolerance practised in China with the religious furies of Europe. Confucius himself is almost beyond praise.

---

[1] *Gesammelte kleine philosophische Schriften*, 1740, vi. 67 ff. See also vi. 529 ff. and *The Real Happiness of a People under a Philosophical King*, 1750.

[2] *The Travels of Cyrus*, 1751, p. 294.

His ethic is as pure, as austere, and at the same time as human as that of Epictetus . . . He enjoins forgiveness of injuries, gratitude for benefits received, friendship, and humanity. His disciples were a community of brothers. The period during which his laws were followed was the happiest and most honourable this earth has ever known.[1]

And now the case for the sceptics must he heard.

e. SCEPTICS

I have included Wolff among the believers because he did not question the Jesuit account of Chinese civilization as wholly admirable. He might have been listed with the sceptics because he sided with the minority view that Confucianism was an atheist and humanist philosophy. Bayle was of the same mind, and this enabled him to reach two conclusions disturbing to the orthodox. First, what has become of the *consensus omnium gentium*, if the oldest and wisest people of Asia was without God? Second, it is clear that revealed religion is not indispensable to morality, not even to a morality that can compare favourably with that of the New Testament.

That there is a knowledge of God among all peoples and at all times—this, remarks Bayle, is as difficult to prove as it is easy to assert. It would require evidence beyond the power of man to assemble. Could it be proved true of all known peoples, are they more than a fraction of the race at one short phase of its history? Think what unexplored regions would need to be investigated, what languages mastered, what strange customs interpreted, before a statement about 'all' men at 'all' times would acquire plausibility. In the case of China, many of those who lived in the country for years and acquired its language report that its scholars are atheists. Others say that the true God was *originally* known there, but they admit that few now retain that knowledge. And Le Gobien, Jesuit as he is, gives an account of the dominant philosophy that makes it sheer materialism.[2]

[1] *Oeuvres*, xv. 275.   [2] *Continuation des Pensées Diverses*, 1705, ii. 537 ff.

To crown his argument, Bayle quotes a letter written by Longobardi in 1598 to the head of his order, in which he dilates on the virtues of the scholar class and regrets only that men of such admirable qualities should be so blind in religion, atheists who deny the immortality of the soul and scout the whole notion of rewards and punishments after death.[1] How is it possible after this to maintain that the dogmas of revealed religion alone can prevent society from breaking down into the war of all against all? Voltaire was to join issue with Bayle on this point. His variety of deism was indispensable to social cohesion and stability. 'To reject outright any belief in God would be an error with frightful moral consequences, an error incompatible with wise government.'[2] He therefore sides with Ricci against Longobardi. Clearly, the dispute was interminable, for there were witnesses waiting to be called on both sides.

Voltaire warned the orthodox critics of the Jesuits that they were playing a dangerous game. But there were those among the orthodox to whom it did not appear that much was at stake. They could not accept the high estimate so many of the missionaries set on the Confucian ethic. In his *Dialogues des Morts* Fenelon, for example, stages a conversation between Socrates and Confucius. The latter admits frankly that he confined himself to a morality of social utility. Socrates replies that he for his part insisted on going back to first principles. Indeed, he doubts whether what Confucius teaches deserves the name of morality. Is it more than social convention? When Confucius replies by citing the travellers who have praised his countrymen, Socrates wants more evidence. There are those who tell a very different story, who say that

of all the people on the face of the earth, the Chinese are the most vain, the most superstitious, the most mercenary, the most unjust, and the biggest liars.[3]

[1] *Continuation des Pensées Diverses*, 1705, ii. 785 f.
[2] *Oeuvres*, xv. 280.   [3] *Oeuvres*, 1835, ii. 571.

47

The China legend was becoming discredited. Grimm could say in 1776:

The Chinese Empire has become in our time the object of special attention and special study. The missionaries first fascinated public opinion by rose-coloured reports from that distant land, too distant to be able to contradict their falsehoods. Then the philosophers took it up, and drew from it whatever could be of use to them in denouncing and removing the evils they observed in their own country. Thus this country became in a short time the home of wisdom, virtue, and good faith, its government the best possible and the longest established, its morality the loftiest and most beautiful in the known world; its laws, its policy, its art, its industry, were likewise such as to serve for a model to all nations of the earth.[1]

[1] Reichwein, op. cit. p. 96.

IV

Rationalism and Romanticism

a. THE EDUCATION OF THE RACE

WE may take a moment now to look back over the way by which we have travelled thus far. We have seen how wider knowledge, first of Islam and then of China, left Europe no alternative but to recognize the presence of truth beyond the frontiers of the Christian religion. The critics of the Church, of course, seized on this evidence with avidity; it did but confirm the conclusion at which they had arrived from a study of classical antiquity. Within the Church, on the other hand, we witnessed the emergence in some quarters of a world-historical perspective. There was a primitive revelation, first to Adam and then to Noah, and while this was virtually lost elsewhere, it had maintained itself in Israel and to a less extent in China. Traces of a *preparatio evangelica* were therefore to be found everywhere. This judgment received support by the publication at Oxford of Thomas Hyde's *Veterum Persarum et Parthorum et Mediorum religionis Historia* (2nd edn. 1760). Hyde suggests that Zoroaster had some knowledge of the Old Testament and had profited by conversation with Jewish exiles. The coming of Messiah was revealed by him, and it was because of this that the Magi were sent by the Persian king of that time to pay homage to him at his birth. God had a peculiar love for this people, because they preserved so much of the original revelation handed on to them through Shem and Elam.

This, then, was the orthodox perspective. The rationalism of the eighteenth century operated with the same materials but produced a different structure. It denied an original revelation

D   49

from which the race had fallen away, and had therefore to work with the hypothesis of a development, truth lying in the future rather than the past. Revelation then became either a claim put forward by the priestly class to secure their own authority or an auxiliary to natural religion. The most important presentation of this view is Lessing's.

Lessing belongs to rationalism by his emphasis on natural religion and his reduction of this to a few simple and immediately acceptable ideas. But he transcends it by his recognition that positive religion is more than priestcraft. It is a historical necessity. His principle is that 'all positive and revealed religions are equally true and equally false'. They are equally true because all alike meet a social need at a particular point in history; equally false because all alike obscure the essential by placing the non-essential on a level with it.[1]

For a fuller statement we turn to *The Education of the Human Race*. An original revelation of the truths that make up natural religion is granted but not stressed. For the universal religion we must look to the future. It is the goal towards which we are being led. And the function of revelation is to get us there sooner than we should have done had we been left to ourselves. It speeds up the process for the race as education does for the individual.

Education gives man nothing which he could not also get from within himself; it gives him that which he could get from within himself, only quicker and more easily. In the same way, too, revelation gives nothing to the human race which human reason could not arrive at on its own; only it has given, and still gives to it, the most important of these things sooner.[2]

The sacred book is part of this process. It is a primer containing the instruction appropriate to each stage of development. The Old Testament taught a religion of rewards and punishments in this world, since only so could the Hebrews be brought one day to

[1] H. Chadwick, *Lessing's Theological Writings*, 1956, pp. 104 f.
[2] Ibid. p. 83.

grasp the unity of God. We Christians have the New Testament as 'the second, better primer for the race of man'.[1] But this is not final. We look for an 'age of the Spirit', a 'new eternal gospel'. Nor is this a mere aspiration. It is a certainty, for progress is inevitable. Or, if not that, it is an article of faith. 'It will assuredly come! the time of a new eternal gospel, which is promised us in the primers of the New Covenant itself.'[2]

It is never easy to interpret Lessing when he writes on religious matters. Just because he knows that what he has to say will disturb, he introduces concessions and modifications that will gain it a hearing. We are probably nearer to what he himself believed in the play *Nathan the Wise*, especially in the parable of the three rings to which the action is meant to lead up. It is Nathan's answer to Saladin's question: Which of the three religions is the true one? In a certain family, a ring has been handed down from generation to generation, each father giving it to the dearest of his sons. It has power to make the wearer loved by God and man. The time comes when a father has three sons who are equally dear and he promises the ring to each. On his deathbed he therefore orders two copies of the original ring and gives one of the three to each of the brothers. After his death, each claims that his is the genuine one and they go to law to settle the dispute. The judge refuses a decision, but offers advice. Let them go away and so live as to demonstrate the virtues of the ring.

> So, free from prejudice, let each one aim
> To emulate his brethren in the strife
> To prove the virtues of his several ring,
> By offices of kindness and of love,
> And trust in God. And if, in years to come,
> The virtues of the ring shall reappear
> Amongst your children's children, then, once more
> Come to this judgment-seat. A greater far
> Than I shall sit upon it, and decide.[3]

[1] H. Chadwick, *Lessing's Theological Writings*, 1956, p. 93.
[2] Ibid. p. 96.   [3] *Nathan the Wise*, trans. E. Bell, 1888, pp. 82 f.

The test is 'By your fruits'. To ask which is the true religion is to ask an idle and a dangerous question. Idle, because no man has the knowledge to answer it; and if appeal is made to revelation, all three, Judaism, Christianity, and Islam can lay claim to this. Dangerous, because that way lie intolerance, fanaticism, subordination of moral integrity to religious zeal, perversion of human relationships, and open strife in the end—all this is developed in the body of the drama. The only question worth asking is which religion does most good, and this only time, tolerance, and concentration on essentials will show. The play makes a special application of this lesson for the benefit of Christians. Let them abandon once for all their claim to a monopoly of the truth. Let them accept their religion as one among several, a historical phenomenon like the others, and live by the human rather than the Christian. The eighteenth century has completed what the seventeenth began, and the missionary perspective has been quite abandoned.

b. HISTORICAL RELATIVISM

The overcoming of rationalism had begun with Lessing, when he formulated the idea of a historical process in which each of the religions had its part to play. But he was not able to develop this, and he fell back in the end on the poverty of natural religion. The next step was taken by Herder in his *Outlines of a Philosophy of the History of Man* (1784-1791), a work that astonishes equally by its detail and its synoptic vision, its recognition that nature conditions man and its confidence that man transcends nature.

The ruling idea of the book is that of the individual as an organic whole, rich in potentialities that develop under the influence of the environment, and in its turn one aspect of a whole of similar nature. What man is is therefore not to be found by penetrating behind the flux of phenomena to some permanent substance; he comes to be what he is in and through these phenomena, in and through the historical process. As to what the individual is that constitutes the unit of history—on this point

Herder is ambiguous. Sometimes it is the individual person, as when he speaks of man as intermediate between two worlds and destined for immortality. Sometimes again it is the nation. But for Herder the nation is a natural community as the state is not. The latter is often a mere product of conquest, whereas the former has a set of innate powers and develops these through a life peculiarly its own. At any given point in its development, it is to be understood as the resultant of two sets of forces, those inherent in it and those brought to bear on it from the environment. Had the European peoples, for example, been set down in less favourable climatic conditions, they would not have reached their present supremacy. Nay more, no one would have known what qualities they possessed, since these can be discerned only as they are expressed in history, and there would have been no such expression.

Each nation has a great part to play, in turn, in the development of man. For man has a vocation to 'humanity', and this is fulfilled only as his potentialities are realized. Critics of Herder complain that he has given no adequate account of what he means by this 'humanity'. I would reply that no such account is in the nature of the case possible. Herder has done all that can be done, so presented the idea that it awakens in us the appropriate response, if we are willing to obey the summons it addresses to us. Fellowship, justice, and religion are the principal components of what is meant. Man is so made that it is natural for him to share life with his fellows; he knows himself to be under obligations that forbid the use of this association for private advantage; and he is conscious of that which transcends him and claims his reverence. The attainment of the goal by the human race requires millenia of trial and effort, and numerous peoples must co-operate if it is to be possible. But sooner or later, in some quarter of the globe, everything human that is possible will become actual.

In this improved programme for the education of the race religion is cast for a most important role. In each people it is that basic response to the Whole out of which, by a process of differentiation, such other forms of expression as art and literature spring. In each people, again, tradition is the bearer of religion, and tradition is the means by which, generation by generation, a people educates itself for its task. Further, the principle of the unique character and worth of the individual must mean that the various religions are not to be judged by standards derived from one of them, our own, but that each is to be appraised simply by asking how it met the needs of its people and its time. For

what one nation holds indispensable to the circle of its thoughts has never entered into the mind of a second, and by a third has been deemed injurious.[1]

To be understood, a religion has to be set against its geographical background and within its historical context. How different this from the abstract natural religion that moderns have invented and foisted upon an equally abstract and invented man! Must we then surrender to relativism? It would seem so.

Singular and wonderful are what we call the genetic spirit and character of a people. It is inexplicable; it is ineradicable; ancient as the nation, ancient as the country he inhabits. The Brahmin pertains to his region: no other, he is persuaded, merits its sacred soil. Thus the Siamese and the Japanese; everywhere, out of their own country, they are untimely planted shrubs. What the Indian solitary thinks of his god, the Siamese of his emperor, we do not think: what to us appear activity and freedom of mind, manly honour and female beauty, in their eyes are far otherwise. . . . It is the same with all the customs of diversified man, nay, with all that appears on our earth.[2]

To know all is therefore to accept all. Every religion is justified in its place, and criticism is ruled out as inapplicable. Christianity is the religion of Europe, Hinduism of India: he who says this has said all there is to say. The wise man will therefore accept the beliefs of others as valid for them. His own are not superior; they are merely those that are appropriate to his situation and so

[1] *Outlines, etc.*, trans. T. Churchill, 1800, p. 201.   [2] Ibid. p. 314.

valid for him. Herder only says clearly what is in the minds of many today.

If a nation or a class of men possess good morals and arts; if it have such ideas and such virtues as suffice for its labours and a happy and contented life; it is sufficiently enlightened for its wants; even supposing it unable to account for an eclipse, otherwise than by the well-known tale of the dragon. . . . I cannot possibly persuade myself that every individual of every nation was intended to acquire a metaphysical idea of God, without which, though probably at last turning on a mere word, he must be superstitious, barbarous, and less than man.[1]

Historical relativism has arrived and it will pursue us to the end of this enquiry. It is difficult to refute, but it is not on that account to be accepted. For the fact is that it just *cannot* be accepted in practice. None of us occupies a standpoint outside the historical process. He is within it and must pass judgment from the position he occupies. Complete suspension of judgment is out of the question. Certainly, it is not to be found in Herder. He condemns China, in spite of his familiarity with the Jesuits and their panegyrics.

The empire is an embalmed mummy, wrapped in silk, and painted with hieroglyphics; its internal circulation is that of a dormouse in its winter sleep.[2]

He finds much to praise in Hinduism, but censures as pernicious the caste system and the practice of suttee. Despotism, polygamy, and servitude to the letter of the Koran, are the charges brought against Islam. The account of Christianity is unhistorical and quite in the spirit of the Enlightenment. He draws a sharp distinction between the religion *of* Christ and the religion *about* him. No praise is too much for the former, no blame too severe for the latter. 'His vital scheme for the welfare of mankind' is opposed to 'an unreflecting adoration' of 'his cross and person'.[3]

[1] *Outlines, etc.*, trans. T. Churchill, 1800 p. 312.
[2] Ibid. p. 296.　　　　　[3] Ibid. p. 492.

Historical relativism has arrived and must be accepted. Yet it must also somehow be overcome. This is the problem with which we shall henceforth be concerned.

c. RELIGION IN ESSENCE AND MANIFESTATION

Herder, we have seen, was still fettered by the rationalist dogma of natural religion to some extent. In Schleiermacher, on the other hand, emancipation was complete. The essence of religion is not to be constructed *a priori* out of abstract ideas such as God, duty, and immorality. It is not the kernel that remains when the husk has been thrown away; it is rather the life that sustains an organism through all its changes. And religion is neither metaphysics nor morals; it is *sui generis*. Since its home is neither in knowing nor in doing, there remains but one possibility, feeling. Whereas in science we are concerned with establishing relations between items within the universe, in religion we have to do with the universe as a whole. Whereas in morality we are active, in religion we are passive. True, religion is bound up with particulars, but not with them *qua* particular. They are doors that open out upon the infinite, points at which the Whole makes impact upon us. So religion is response in feeling to the infinite as it offers itself to us in and through the finite. I quote the famous paragraph from the *Speeches*, for it is with this initial phase in Schleiermacher's thinking that we are here concerned.

The contemplation of the pious is the immediate consciousness of the universal existence of all finite things, in and through the Infinite, and of all temporal things in and through the Eternal. Religion is to seek this and find it in all that lives and moves, in all growth and change, in all doing and suffering. It is to have life and to know life in immediate feeling, only as such an existence in the Infinite and Eternal. Where this is found, religion is satisfied, where it hides itself there is for her unrest and anguish, extremity and death. Wherefore it is a life in the infinite nature of the Whole, in the One and in the All, having and possessing all things in God, and God in all.[1]

[1] John Oman, *Schleiermacher on Religion*, 1893, p. 36.

The Romantic principle of individuality now receives a two-fold application. In the first place, since each person is a unique individual, each will appreciate and respond to the universe in his own way. There will be as many ways to God as there are souls whom he has made. In the second place, each of the religions is an individual whole, an unique evaluation of the universe in feeling. So the common essence of religion is manifest in a rich variety of forms. Each religion is an apprehension of the Whole from a particular perspective; what other perspectives yield will not be absent from it, but will be subordinate within it. Or, to use other language, religion-as-such consists of a number of elements that can take on any pattern. Each positive religion is one such pattern, and in each some one element occupies a central and determining position. Each tends

> to select some one of the great relations of mankind to the Highest Being, and, in a definite way, make it the centre and refer to it all the others. . . . By every formation of this kind one of the endless number of different views and different arrangements of the single elements, which are all possible and all require to be fully exhibited, is fully realized.[1]

From this it would seem to follow that all religions are equally true. Or rather, that the distinction between truth and falsehood does not apply to religions. Schleiermacher says as much. But we soon see that this refers, not at all to the actual religions, but only to the feeling-responses out of which they arise.

> All is immediately true in religion, for except immediately how could anything arise? But that only is immediate, which has not yet passed through the stage of idea, but has grown up merely in the feeling. All that is religious is good, for it is only religious as it expresses a common higher life.[2]

Doctrine is the product of reflection upon feeling, and as such may be mistaken. Hence any actual religion, Christianity included, will be a mixture of truth and error.

[1] John Oman, *Schleiermacher on Religion*, 1893, p. 223.　　[2] Ibid. p. 54.

What then is the place of Christianity among the religions? We are told that it is 'the religion of religions', the positive religion that realizes, as no other does, what all religion is meant to be. If we ask where this religion is to be found, we are directed to Christ. He not merely enunciated the Christian idea, he embodied it. So doing, he created a religion. At the same time, he formed a school to continue it. But these two are not to be confused. 'He never maintained that he was the only mediator, the only one in whom his idea actualized itself.'[1] The name 'Christian' may be given, it would seem, to anyone who thinks in terms of man's corruption and his redemption by God, even though he does not connect these with Christ.

Precisely because Christianity is of this order, derived from Christ but not identical with him, because it sees all things, itself included, as shot through with human weakness yet sustained by divine power, it can face the future with confidence though without arrogance.

As long as our age endures, nothing disadvantageous to Christianity can come forth, whether from the age or from Christianity itself, and from all strife and battle it must issue renewed and glorified.[2]

We might suppose this to imply that it will eventually displace the other religions. But this is not Schleiermacher's intention. As long as the world stands, we may expect that they will survive and flourish alongside our own. Indeed, new faiths may appear. For 'as nothing is more irreligious than to demand general uniformity in mankind, so nothing is more unchristian than to seek uniformity in religion'.[3]

So much for the *Speeches*. The conclusion is an indecisive one. The question is raised again in *The Christian Faith*. We meet there a new definition of the essence of religion. It lies now in 'the feeling of absolute dependence'. But the various religions are still regarded as species of one genus.

[1] John Oman, *Schleiermacher on Religion*, 1893, p. 248.
[2] Ibid. p. 267.   [3] Ibid. p. 252.

In every individual religion the God-consciousness which in itself remains the same everywhere on the same level, is attached to some relation of the self-consciousness in such an especial way that only thereby can it unite with other determinations of the self-consciousness; so that all other relations are subordinate to this one, and it communicates to all others its colour and its tone.[1]

Religions are classified as aesthetic and teleological, the former predominantly natural and the latter predominantly ethical. Islam, surprisingly enough, is classed as aesthetic because it enjoins submission to Allah's inscrutable will. What distinguishes Christianity is 'that in it everything is related to the redemption accomplished by Jesus of Nazareth'. That is to say, emphasis now passes from his 'idea' to his person and work.

In Jesus the God-consciousness was entire and unbroken, as his life was sinless. He can redeem others because he does not himself need redemption. Therefore there can be no talk of other mediators along with him. Indeed, 'in comparison with him, everything which could otherwise be regarded as revelation again loses this character'.[2]

Christianity is therefore superior to all its rivals. One day it 'will be able to extend itself over the whole human race'. Not that it will supersede other faiths: it will bring them to fulfilment by taking up into itself whatever truth they contain. As it preserves today what was of permanent value in Hebrew faith and Greek wisdom, so it will be enriched eventually from the treasures of India and China. Then 'all religions will be visible in Christianity'.[3] This carries with it another departure from the earlier position. Missionary activity is now permissible. For, while in the deepest sense there is but one religious communion to which each faith makes its contribution, at the same time, as far as the empirical religions are concerned, some are higher and others lower. They form a graded series, and it is the duty of those who stand higher to invite those who stand lower to climb

[1] *The Christian Faith*, 1928, p. 47. [2] Ibid. p. 63.
[3] Oman, op. cit. p. 108.

up and join them. They will not lose by so doing, for the new religion is hospitable to everything in the old that was of abiding worth. What is not justified is the impatience and intolerance that would sweep away the old entirely. He who commends his own religion to another should do so as one partner in the life of the spirit speaking to another.

d. APPEAL TO REVELATION

Without an absolute man cannot live, and in religion he knows himself claimed by an absolute. Yet, when he looks out upon the variety of religions known to history, he finds no absolute. Each religion is relative, conditioned by a particular setting. This is the problem that has emerged. Schleiermacher has outlined a solution to it that will be filled in by Hegel. Granted that a hierarchy of religions can be conceived, it is then permissible to think that the highest in the series completes and fulfils all those below it, and that these, when they have discharged each its mission, are meant to lose themselves—and also to find themselves—in the one enduring religion. But before we consider this, we must turn aside to consider another approach to the problem, and that a distinctively Christian and Catholic one.

Friedrich Schlegel had one great advantage over most of those we have considered hitherto, in that he possessed a first-hand knowledge of Indian language and literature. He learned Sanskrit while in Paris during the Napoleonic War, his teacher being an Englishman detained there by the outbreak of hostilities. His brother August Wilhelm caught the enthusiasm from him and held the first chair of Sanskrit in a German university. He translated the Gita into Latin and began, though he did not complete, an edition of the Ramayana.

Friedrich Schlegel's philosophy of history falls within his Catholic period; it is therefore overtly Christian throughout. Christ is the centre of history in more than a chronological sense. What preceded was a preparation for him; what follows bears his impress even where he is rejected; and the future is hopeful just in so far as it promises a return to his guidance. World-history as a whole is governed by the departure, as far as the major portion of the race is concerned, from a primitive revelation, coupled with the preservation of this among the Hebrews and also, in fragmentary and mythological form, among some other peoples, till the advent of Christ and the new turn in the process that comes with him.

Man is constituted man by the divine word, the communication from God that enables him to know and serve him and at the same time binds him to his fellows in moral opportunity and obligation. But already in Adam man lost the blessed relation to God in which he was meant to stand. This, however, belongs rather to the prelude to history than to history proper. The latter begins with the first rivalry, the first murder. Here Schlegel follows Augustine. History is the conflict between two cities, two states of mind, between the children of Seth and the children of Cain.

This opposition and this discord—this hostile struggle between the two great divisions of the human race, forms the whole tenure of primitive history. When the moral harmony of man had once been deranged, and two opposite wills had sprung up within him, a divine will or a will seeking God, and a natural will or a will bent on sensible objects, passionate and ambitious, it is easy to conceive how mankind from their very origin must have diverged into two opposite paths.[1]

The two races, as they appear in the early phases of history, are the patriarchs, lovers of God and custodians of the ancient tradition and the giants and demigods of Scripture and myth, arrogant and hostile to God. The memory of this primal conflict has been preserved in every nation, in however fabulous a form.

Here then is the yard-stick by which the various religions are to be measured. We must ask in each case how much it has preserved of the primitive revelation. After Israel, the first place is assigned to Zoroastrianism, which

[1] *Philosophy of History*, 1846, p. 97.

deserves to rank next to the Christian faith and doctrine, as propounded in the Old Testament and developed and completed in the New: its severe truth and high moral tendency give it a decided superiority to all other Oriental systems.[1]

Zoroaster is not to be regarded as the founder of the religion; he did but hand on and recast a tradition of remote antiquity.

India comes next. The *rishis* of the Vedas, Brahmins by birth, correspond to the Hebrew patriarchs. After Adam's reconciliation with God he handed on to Seth the truth and powers he had received, and the Brahmin caste, degenerate as it is today, springs from Seth's descendants by one line as a class of men 'chosen by God, and entirely devoted to his service'.[2] In the belief in transmigration the memory of the Fall still works obscurely upon man. He knows himself so estranged from God that only long discipline and purgation can bring him back to him.

The worst instance of the descent into superstition that charaterizes all history except that of the chosen people, is, however, China.

Among the great nations of antiquity who stood the nearest or at least, very near, to the source of sacred tradition—the word of primitive revelation—the Chinese hold a very distinguished place; and many passages in their primitive history, many remarkable vestiges of eternal truth—the heritage of old thoughts—to be found in their ancient classical works, prove the originally high eminence of this people. But at a very early period, their science had taken a course completely erroneous, and even their language partly followed this direction, or at least assumed a very still and artificial character. Descending from one degree of political idolatry to a grade still lower, they have at last openly embraced a foreign superstition—a diabolical mimicry of Christianity, which emanated from India, has made Thibet its principal seat, prevails in China, and, widely diffused over the whole middle of Asia, reckons a greater number of followers than any other religion on the earth.[3]

---

[1] *Aesthetic and Miscellaneous Works*, 1849, p. 485.
[2] *Philosophy of History*, p. 150.   [3] Ibid. p. 137.

Islam, of course, meets with unqualified condemnation. What else was possible in the case of a religion that represented for Schlegel not merely the loss of a primitive revelation, but the rejection of the full light of truth?

Schlegel's voice is that of one crying in the wilderness. He thinks in terms of degeneration while his contemporaries were writing 'Progress' on their banner. The future lies with the idea of development, with explanation by the *terminus ad quem* rather than by the *terminus a quo*. So we come to Hegel.

V

The Way of the Absolute

a. HEGEL

HEGEL's starting-point was a vision of reality as one and spiritual. It both is such and becomes such. Indeed, it only is such in the process of becoming such, as it only becomes such because it eternally is such. Spirit is the origin, the way, and the goal of the supreme and all-inclusive adventure. What we first greet in its most abstract form as pure Being passes through transformation after transformation till it reveals itself in the end as the self-consciousness that is both Subject and Object, that than which nothing can be more concrete. Spirit can come to itself through a series of phases just because it is already present in each. And if we ask whether the development is historical, with phase succeeding phase in time, or logical, so that we could infer any one of the phases from what went before it, the answer is that both accounts are correct. It is in 'history comprehended conceptually' that Absolute Spirit comes into its own.

The point at which this happens, at which the Absolute comes to awareness of itself and its journey hitherto, is man. He is that phase of the Absolute which apprehends the development. The pilgrim, as it were, reaches the point at which he sees the shrine towards which he travels and begins to understand that the pilgrimage has all the while been within himself. But, though the Absolute attains in man to knowledge of itself, that knowledge is not yet absolute. In art, it apprehends itself through sense-objects and therefore only obscurely. In religion it does so by representation, picture and image and symbol. Only in philosophy, that 'thinking upon thought' which Aristotle judged divine, is absolute knowledge reached. So the content is the same in philosophy and religion; the expression differs. Where, for example, religion speaks of God creating the world, philosophy describes how the Idea goes out of itself to become other than itself, that it may finally return to itself.

On this view, the essence of religion can be defined in two ways—and these two are one. It is at once Spirit aware of itself in man and man aware of himself as spirit. These are what Hegel calls the moments of universality and particularity respectively in religion. They are reconciled in the third moment, that of worship. So religion can be described with equal truth as God coming to himself in man and as man coming to himself in God. He who worships knows himself to be one with God. 'Worship is thus, in fact, the eternal process by which the subject posits itself as identical with its essential being.'[1] The centre of religion is the *unio mystica*. But this unity requires to be approached through the separation that preceded it. Man comes to himself in God because he has been reconciled to him, because the alienation between them has now been overcome. He sees in God the other who is at the same time himself. That is to say, he repudiates the empirical self that stood over against God as the finite over against the infinite, and apprehends God as the unity of finite and infinite. The final insight therefore is that God and man are one though they are not the same. For the Absolute only is through the relativities in which it comes to expression.

It has been necessary to devote so much space to the general pattern of Hegel's thinking to make it clear that we have now to do with an exceptionally promising attempt to grapple with that problem of how to combine the relativities of history with the absolute of devotion which, once raised, cannot henceforth be set aside. To each movement in the self-development of Spirit there corresponds an awareness of this in accordance with the possibilities of that stage, in other words, a particular religion.

[1] *Philosophy of Religion*, English and Foreign Philosophical Library, 1895, i. 70.

Each of these is true in its place, and a higher stage contains a fuller truth than a lower. Yet none of them is the true religion. That only comes at the final stage, in the religion that takes up into itself and brings to fulfilment all that went before. Christianity therefore supersedes all other faiths because it justifies them. Each of them apprehended the unity of God and man to the extent that this was possible at its point in the process. What was obscurely grasped in them becomes actual in it.

The stages through which religion passes are three in number. In the first Spirit is as it were asleep, in the second it wakes and moves, in the third it comes to full self-consciousness. For the religions of nature (those of China and India) God is substance and impersonal power, for those of spiritual individuality (Greece, Rome, and Israel) he is free and personal over against man, for the absolute religion (Christianity) he becomes man and so effects the reconciliation that makes God and man one. These stages are like the childhood, youth, and manhood of a person; as an adult he looks back and sees how in the earlier phases he was coming to himself without being fully aware of what was taking place. Each of the three groups again contains within itself three distinct religions or, in the last instance, the three forms under which God reveals himself, as Father, as Son, and as Spirit.

Christianity is at once ideal and actual. It is both God's self-consciousness and an institution within the world, both the last in the series of religions and the truth of all religions. As such, it is *absolute*. It is not possible that it should be surpassed. Beyond it, nothing more remains in the sphere of religion. Christianity is as it were the answer to the prayers offered by the religions, the fulfilment of their aspirations. It exposes their shortcomings only that it may demonstrate how even these were pointers to the truth it brings. It is also *revealed*. This must not be understood in the popular sense, as though it were a set of truths communicated to men by God. Revelation is its very nature. Now at last the religious spirit knows what it has been seeking down the ages. Now at last, to say the same thing in other words, God attains to full self-consciousness. 'The absolute religion is the *revealed* religion, the religion which has itself for its content, its fulness.'[1]

It is an imposing and splendid construction. But is it a convincing one? I shall have something to say on that in the sequel. Here it will suffice to borrow a leaf from Hegel's book and say that it was historically justified and *therefore* destined to be superseded. It bears the impress of a time when Europe had as yet only such contacts with and knowledge of the East as confirmed it in its own sense of superiority. It did not yet doubt that its standards were those by which all else should be judged, that its civilization represented the climax of historical development, though it could graciously admit that others were not without their value. But an obscure *Private-dozent* in Berlin was to launch against all this self confidence his counter-attack from the East.

b. MYTH AND REVELATION

Before we turn to Schopenhauer, we can take time to consider how another representative of Absolute Idealism reached the same conclusion by a somewhat different path. It will not be necessary here to trace the development of Schelling's thought, or, as some would say, to follow the various aberrations in which he indulged. I shall confine myself to the *Philosophie der Mythologie* and the *Philosophie der Offenbarung*, both of which were published posthumously. There is evidence in both these works that he had taken pains to master the literature available on the various religions, both ancient and modern, as also that he was prepared at times to risk a judgment where he was not qualified to offer one. Extravagant and unconvincing as much of the detail in the former series of lectures is, it rendered great service by its insistence that myth is not to be dismissed as mere fantasy-thinking, but deserves to be taken seriously for the truth it yields. It is the work of mind, though not its deliberate creation. In mythical thinking, as in logical, there is commerce between

[1] *Philosophy of Religion*, English and Foreign Philosophical Library, 1895, ii. 330.

subject and object. There is that in nature which can be grasped by conceptual thought, but there is that which lies deeper, to be expressed indeed in image and story, but in image and story as vehicles for truth.

The mythological process has arisen in man independently of his wishes and thoughts. . . . Mythology is a natural, a necessary growth. . . . Mythology is essentially active and self-moving in accordance with an indwelling law. It is actually the highest human consciousness that is stirring in myth, and through the very contradictions in which it involves itself and which none the less it surmounts, it proves that it is something real, true, and necessary.[1]

As we should put it today, mythology is a product of the collective unconscious and therefore given, authoritative, and illuminating for the individual consciousness. The objects with which it deals belong to the reality of the psyche.

This view of myth was nothing short of epoch-making. Myth is neither to be scouted as priestly fiction nor evaporated into general moral principles. Nor are the figures that appear in it mere personifications of natural forces. For primitive peoples do not project their own mental states upon a dead nature, they experience nature as a realm of forces akin to themselves. They do not, as we do, reduce nature to a complex of things while reserving for themselves what is felt about things. That the sky lowers and the rock menaces are for them qualities of the sky and the rock.

Schelling puts it that divine potencies are at work in nature, so that natural religion in the proper sense of the term will be man's encounter with these forces in nature and in himself. The original unity of the divine life includes within itself the interaction of three potencies. They set up in God a condition of unrest from which he escapes by externalizing them in the creation of the world. In man these potencies attain to equilibrium, yet the maintenance of that equilibrium depends thereafter on his

[1] Quoted in Cassirer, *The Problem of Knowledge*, Oxford University Press, 1950, p. 297.

freedom, and in freedom he chooses to disturb it. So once again the condition of 'unblessedness' appears in the divine life. The process must therefore begin all over again. God must come to his own once more, this time in the human race and in particular in its religious development. Here we see repeated in time the process that belongs to God's eternity. The religious development of the race is at the same time a theogony, the coming to be of God as immanent in his creation. The religions of the world in their successive stages yield a history of divine revelation only to be understood out of the depths of God's own being.

Thus Schelling has broken entirely with the notion of natural religion as a set of general truths and reached an appreciation of it as experience, encounter with the divine. There is a dealing of God with man in all the history of the race, as all our search for him falls within the context of his self-revelation. In the second of the two works with which we are concerned, he makes clear that revelation is not another term for discovery. It is not the crown of man's development nor the flower of his religious experiences. It is something new. Man cannot give it to himself or find it for himself. He must receive it from God. Its content is not to be known in advance, it cannot even be inferred from the mythological process that preceded it. It is the self-disclosure of God in freedom as personal. It is beyond reason yet not irrational. To speak of it as 'the education of the human race' is quite inadequate. For man needs more than education, he needs reconciliation. This revelation brings to him, revelation as event.

The characteristic element which requires to be explained is just the historical. The principal content of Christianity is just Christ himself; not what he said, but what *he is* and did. Christianity is not, in the first place, a doctrine; it is a fact, something objective, and the doctrine can never be anything but the expression of this *fact*.[1]

Unfortunately, Schelling's practice did not accord with his profession. He got entangled in a morass of Gnostic theosophy. When he tells us that his aim is not 'to construct a speculative

[1] Quoted in Pfleiderer, *Philosophy of Religion*, 1897, ii. 16.

dogmatic system', but 'to explain Christianity out of its higher historical context', we wonder where the difference lies.

What then has Schelling to say on the relation between Christianity and other religions? He is aware of the importance of the question in view of increasing contact between East and West, as also of its bearing on the missionary enterprise. The missionary, he tells us, fails because he dismisses heathenism as false and imposes in its place doctrinal formulations far beyond the grasp of the convert. Christ should be presented, not as the negation of the great ethnic faiths, but as their fulfilment. The coming of Christ is that wholly new event—here justice is done to what is meant by revelation—that at once exposes the error in what went before and satisfies its aspirations.

A religion that was not in being from the origin of the world and throughout all times cannot be the true one. Christianity must therefore have been present in heathenism also; the latter has in substance the same content. Or, as I put the same thought earlier: Christ was in heathenism—only not as Christ. That is what I meant by saying 'in substance' and not 'in his truth'.[1]

Christ, that is to say, was present in every age to every race, but he was not yet known as such. Heathenism is related to Christianity as law to gospel, reason to faith, nature to grace. The heathen is like a blind man, feeling the sun's warmth but not seeing the sun itself. Christ was within heathenism as natural potency but not yet as personal principle.

We detect the influence of the German mystics, an influence that was at work already in Hegel but is much more evident in Schelling. We are reminded of Sebastian Franck. Christ is 'the light that lighteth every man that cometh into the world'. There is the possibility here of an advance on Hegel's position, inasmuch as we can envisage the fulfilment of human hopes in a person and not merely in an idea. We shall have to return in due course to this theme of the Christ who is at work in the world under two forms, latent in one and manifest in the other.

[1] *Werke*, iv/2. 77.

VI

Counter-attack from the East

a. THE EAST ARRIVES

SCHOPENHAUER represents a turning-point in the relation between Western and Eastern thought. Hitherto, the representatives of the former did not for a moment doubt the superiority of their heritage or their right to judge the rest of the world by their standards. Now, however, a thinker appears who cites the Vedas equally with Plato, confirms by appeal to the Buddhist scriptures what he learned from Kant, and regards the true in Christianity as substantially identical with what it has in common with Hinduism and Buddhism, the false as those points at which it differs from them. The book that captivated him was Anquetil Hyacinthe Du Perron's translation of the Upanishads. He spoke of the 'profound, lofty, and original thoughts' to be found on every page of this, as of the 'high and holy seriousness' that characterized it as a whole.

It is the most rewarding and the most elevating reading (the original excepted) the world has to offer. It has been the consolation of my life and will be my consolation when I come to die.[1]

Du Perron (1731-1805) enlisted as a private soldier for service in India to enable him to study Oriental languages there. Friends intervened to secure him a post at Pondicherry, and he learned Persian, Sanskrit, Zēnd, and Pehlevi there and elsewhere in India. Returning to Europe, he published in 1771 a translation

[1] *Parerga und Paralipomena*, 1888, ii. 427.

of the Zend Avesta, to be followed in 1801-2 by a Latin rendering of the Upanishads. This was made, not from the Sanskrit original, but from two manuscripts of the Persian version by Prince Bara Shukoh, brother of Aurengzeb.

The title of the book is *Oupnek'hat* (*id est, Secretum Tegendum*), and the original is described as *opus ipsa in India rarissimum*. It runs to two volumes, each of more than 800 pages. The first volume has a preface, giving some account of how the translation came to be made. Then follow quotations, principally from classical and Indian authors, in support of the author's claim that the sacred books of the various ancient peoples agree in affirming one spiritual principle behind the universe. After this comes a collection of passages from Christian authors, beginning with Synesius of Cyrene, in which ideas akin to those in the Upanishads are found. Jewish writers are also laid under contribution. His conclusion is that 'for the wise man there is nothing new; it is simply that one thing is earlier and another later. Nothing is absolutely bad; what is evil either preserves a trace of the good or contains some germ of it'.[1] Six Upanishads are then translated and the rest of the volume—amounting to one half —is given over to notes and emendations plus various supplements, a veritable farrago of learning such as suited the taste of those days. The second volume is of the same miscellaneous character and brings the number of Upanishads up to fifty. The text is a mixture of Latin, Persian, and Sanskrit, with the Greek definite article thrown in from time to time.

That Schopenhauer was able to learn so much from a hotch-potch of this kind is amazing. He could scarcely have done so without the guidance of scholars such as Jones and Colebrooke.[2] Yet, though he had no knowledge of Sanskrit, he was sufficiently enamoured of Du Perron's work to judge all subsequent translations far inferior.

[1] Op. cit. i. p. cix.
[2] Sir William Jones (1746-94), translated *Sakantula* and *The Laws of Manu*. Thomas Henry Colebrooke (1765-1837), 'the real founder of Indian philology and archaeology' (Winternitz).

It is my fixed conviction that a genuine knowledge of the Upanishads and therefore of the true and esoteric dogmatic of the Vedas is up to now obtainable only through the *Oupnekhat;* one can read through the other translations and have no idea what it is all about.[1]

b. THE WORLD AS WILL

The attraction of Indian thought for Schopenhauer was that it provided a sanction for the metaphysic he derived from Plato and Kant. He could cite a more venerable authority than either Greece or Germany. For, like Plato and Kant, Schopenhauer reduces the world of everyday experience to the status of mere appearance. That which truly *is*, is not to be found there. Instead, we are fobbed off with a flux of phenomena, banished to a realm of which no knowledge is possible but only opinion. Nothing, says Kant, can be known to us save as it has first been operated upon by the mind. Nothing here below, Plato tells us, is more than a copy and shadow of that other world which alone *is*, while everything with us merely becomes. This world is illusion and such knowledge as it yields were better termed opinion. So stated, what could be nearer to the Indian concept of Maya? Take, for example, the following quotation:

> The worlds gained as a result of action, from the plane of Brahma to that of the lowest organism, whether subtle or gross, belong to *samsara*, or the relative universe. Like seed and tree, these worlds are bound by the law of cause and effect and are mutually related. They are beset with a hundred thousand troubles and are insubstantial, like the pith of a plantain tree. They are illusory, like objects conjured up by magic, like the water of a mirage, like a castle in the air, or like dreams. They are unstable, like foam and bubbles.[2]

How eagerly Schopenhauer fastens on this support!

[1] *Parerga etc.* ii. 428.
[2] Nikhilananda, *The Upanishads*, London: Phoenix House, 1951, pp. 276 f.

The Vedas and Puranas have no better simile than a dream for the whole knowledge of the actual world, which they call the web of Maya, and they use none more frequently.[1]

So much for the phenomenal world. What then of the noumenal? For Schopenhauer, the reality behind appearances in one and of the nature of will. The will covers inanimate as well as animate nature; it is the blind, restless, insatiable, driving force of which everything in time and space is but the appearance. The *principium individuationis*, the mistaken belief that each individual existent is a distinct entity with full claim to reality—this is the snare of Maya. And that all life is one—is not this the message of the East? Again and again Schopenhauer reverts to the Upanishads with their slogan of 'the one and all'. To be sure, the reality there is not will; rather does it lie beyond all categories. In Schopenhauer the activism of the West leagues itself with the monism of the East. He is fascinated by the formula in which the ultimate insight comes to expression: 'That art thou.' We might equate the will in Schopenhauer with the *karma* of Hinayana Buddhism, for this is the driving-force that urges men on from desire to desire, from life to life, and therefore leaves them always restless and unhappy.

Granted such a metaphysic, the ethic to be deduced from it is clear. Egoism is evil, altruism good. The sin of sins is to repudiate the basic unity of things, this solidarity of oneself with all that lives and breathes, and to assert one's own claims at the expense of others. Here accordingly Schopenhauer joins hands with Buddhism.

Boundless compassion for all living beings is the surest and most certain guarantee of pure moral conduct, and needs no casuistry. Whoever is filled with it will assuredly injure no one, do harm to no one, encroach on no man's rights; he will rather have regard for every one, forgive every one, help every one as far as he can, and all his actions will bear the stamp of justice and loving-kindness.[2]

[1] *The World as Will and Idea*, London: Routledge & Kegan Paul, 1906, i. 21.
[2] *The Basis of Morality*, trans. A. B. Bullock, London: Allen & Unwin, pp. 213 f.

The good man identifies himself with his fellows, because he is in fact one with them and not the separate individual he once imagined himself to be. The unity of compassion is grounded in the unity of being. Ordinarily, we divide mankind into a vast number of individuals, each with his claims and counter-claims, and among these we naturally give precedence to ourselves. Hence we seek frantically for what will promote our happiness, we envy others, we take offence at what they say or do, and so on. In all this, we are victims of the illusion of multiplicity, we take to be separate and conflicting things what are in reality but so many appearance of the one and all. The possibility of unselfish conduct arises only when we awake from this dream to realize that you and I are not different, we are ultimately one. I love my neighbour because I realize that in the last resort he is myself in disguise.

How, otherwise and metaphysically, are we to account for even the smallest offering of alms made with absolutely no other object than that of lessening the want which afflicts a fellow-creature? Such an act is only conceivable, only possible, in so far as the giver *knows* that it is his very self which stands before him, clad in the garments of suffering; in other words, so far as he recognises the essential part of his own being, under a form *not his own*.[1]

What unites the ethic to the metaphysic is, we now see, a judgment of value. Buddhism and Schopenhauer join in asserting that 'all life is suffering'. If we, our fellows, and the world in which we live are but so many appearances of an unconscious, insatiable will, then we are indeed the sport of gods, if not of a power even less responsible. Such happiness as we enjoy is a brief respite snatched from pain, and our enjoyment of it is vitiated by the realization that pain will soon return, and in a still worse form.

The instruction which his life offers to every one consists, as a whole, in this, that the objects of his desire continually delude, waver, and fall,

[1] *The Basis of Morality*, trans. A. B. Bullock, London: Allen & Unwin, p. 278.

and accordingly bring more misery than joy, till at last the whole foundation upon which they all stand gives way.[1]

This is indeed 'the worst of all possible worlds'. For 'it is so arranged as to be able to maintain itself with great difficulty; but if it were a little worse, it could no longer maintain itself'.[2]

The human predicament being so desperate, the one question worth asking is: What must I do to be saved? Moral conduct provides at least a means of alleviating this immense suffering. But it is never more than a palliative. There are ways of escape open to some, notably art, which withdraws us from participation in the tragedy of life and enables us for a brief while to contemplate it as disinterested spectators. But this is no more than an occasional consolation. Salvation is possible for him only who can deny and destroy the will. So Buddha preached long ago, and the West must go to school with him. True, Christendom has had its saints, its mystics, and its ascetics. But what is their spiritual heroism in comparison with that of the East? Our most ardent deniers of the will do not, like Indian devotees, throw themselves over precipices, bury themselves alive, or fling themselves beneath the car of Juggernaut in an ecstasy of liberation.

What is the goal to be reached by denial of the will? It is the Nirvana of the Buddhist. But how define this? Is it annihilation? Or is it bliss unspeakable? Schopenhauer would say that all depends upon the perspective from which it is viewed. For us who cling to life, the prospect appals. We see it as extinction, the loss of everything to which we cling so eagerly. But if we could call back for a moment those who have actually attained, how different their language would be! We can see as much from the serenity, the purity and calm that are characteristic of them, wherever in the world they appear and whatever religion they profess. They would speak of emancipation, of release from the urgencies of time and the constrictions of space, of a condition no words can describe, because in it all words have been abolished.

[1] *The World, etc.* iii. 384.　　　　[2] Ibid. iii. 395.

c. EX ORIENTE LUX

It is easy from all this to guess how Schopenhauer will judge Christianity. The Indian religions provide him with a standard; that in Christianity which agrees with them will be true, where it departs from them it will be in error. And he understands this even in the sense of historical derivation. In religion, as in philosophy, all light is from the East. So

the New Testament . . . must be in some way traceable to an Indian source: its ethical system, its ascetic view of morality, its pessimism, and its Avatar, are all thoroughly Indian.[1]

The world-view of the Gospels, on this showing, is that of the Upanishads and the Dhammapada: a deep sense of the misery of the world, suffering as the universal inescapable lot, and renunciation as the sole way of salvation. The command of Jesus to the rich young ruler, 'Sell all that thou hast and give to the poor', might well have come from Buddha. To be sure, the Christianity of today has come to terms with the world. But in so doing it has been false to its origins.

But the corruption of Christianity is no recent event. In fact, it is tainted at the source. The Jewish strain in Christianity is responsible for all the evil in it. For Judaism was an optimistic religion; it pronounced the world of nature good and gave its blessing to human life. Its morality was optimistic: 'Increase and multiply!' The material world is real and God discloses himself through history. In all these respects, it is the antithesis of Indian spirituality. Historical Christianity is the result of the fusion of two creeds that originally had nothing in common. The Old Testament is Schopenhauer's bête noire. The superiority of the Oriental religions lies in the fact that they are not contaminated by its absurd belief in the devil, its denial of rights to animals, and its childish appeal to history. Though the New Testament may appear to agree with the Old on such points, the fact rather is

[1] *Complete Essays*, London: Allen & Unwin, iii, 92.

that the doctrines of the Old Testament are rectified and their meaning changed by those of the New, so that, in the most important and essential matters, an agreement is brought about between them and the old religions of India. Everything which is true in Christianity may also be found in Brahmanism and Buddhism.[1]

To this repudiation of the Old Testament there is, however, one exception. The story in Genesis iii is the one suggestion in the Old Testament that the world is what Schopenhauer sees it to be, a vale of tears and misery.

The sole thing that reconciles me to the Old Testament is the story of the Fall. In my eyes, it is the only metaphysical truth in that book, even though it appears in the form of an allegory. There seems to me no better explanation of our existence than that it is the result of some false step, some sin of which we are paying the penalty.[2]

To be sure, India has a better explanation of this. The primal fault was not man's but God's!

Brahma is said to have produced the world by a kind of fall or mistake; and in order to atone for his folly, is bound to remain in it himself till he works out its redemption. As an account of the origin of things, that is admirable![3]

To many Western minds, Indian religion is burdened by one great absurdity, its doctrine of metempsychosis. How does Schopenhauer meet this objection? He has two answers. The first, as he himself points out, has affinities with the denial in Hinayana of any substantial and permanent self. The individual is but an appearance under some form of the all-pervading will. At death, what happens is that the will discards one appearance to assume another. Since the intellect perishes with the body, there is continuity of life without continuity of memory.

---

[1] *Complete Essays,* London: Allen & Unwin, iii. 94.
[2] Ibid. v. 13 f.   [3] Ibid. v. 11 f.

These constant new births, therefore, constitute the succession of the life-dreams of a will which in itself is indestructible, until, instructed and improved by so much and so various successive knowledge in a constantly new form, it abolishes or abrogates itself.[1]

The second reply to the objector is that metempsychosis is a mythological version of what is taught in the Upanishads—that all life is one and that while apparently doer and sufferer are different persons they are ultimately the same. The West has its parallel mythology in the Christian dogma of original sin.

So Hegel's grandiose demonstration of Christianity as the absolute religion is swept aside. It must begin with shame to take a lower place among the religions than those that derive from India.

d. REVISION

The irrationalism of Schopenhauer meant a decisive break with the Hegelian tradition. He would construct no system into which each religion neatly fitted. Nor, indeed, was he interested in religions other than those of India. His follower, Hartmann, went back to Hegel, in part because wider interests compelled a more comprehensive treatment. Between Schopenhauer and Hartmann the situation had been changed radically by the emergence of the science of religion, a new and objective approach with which the name of Max Müller will always be connected. The aim was now not to formulate conclusions but to amass knowledge. The sacred books of the East must be studied and translated, its civilizations understood from within, and judgment resolutely postponed till the facts are in. For the purposes of the new science, the presupposition must be that all religions have equal rights.

The student of Comparative Theology therefore can claim no privilege, no exceptional position of any kind, for his own religion,

[1] *The World*, etc. iii. 300.

whatever that religion may be. For his purposes all religions are natural and historical.[1]

As a believer, of course, the same person may assert that his own religion is superior or all-inclusive, and Max Müller himself could speak thus of his own undogmatic version of Christianity. But a confession of faith is not of the same order as a scientific conclusion.

In the light of the new investigations, it became clear how slender was the basis for the judgments passed by the philosophers. In the first volume of the Gifford Lectures, Max Müller tells how, as a student at Berlin, he attended Schelling's lectures on mythology and found that they 'opened many new views' to his mind. But he was aware, from his study of the Oriental languages, how faulty Schelling's information was on many points and knew him well enough to tell him so. At his request he translated for him some of the Upanishads. When he came to England later, it was with warm commendations from Schelling. Müller tells also of a conversation with Schopenhauer in Frankfort, in which he tried in vain to convince him that a study of the Vedas was necessary if one wished to understand the Upanishads. The philosopher rated them as so much 'priestly rubbish'.[2]

Precisely because he was open to the new knowledge, Hartmann aspired to renew the attempt of Hegel to trace the development of the religious consciousness as an aspiration after the Absolute. To begin with it is embedded in nature. The gods are powers of nature and man worships them because he seeks from them the fulfilment of hopes and desires that are still of the order of nature. But with increasing rationalization and socialization the gods become detached from nature and achieve a measure of spirituality. In Greece and Rome supremely, they take on human form, are organized after the pattern of human society, and take their places within a theology that is designed to systematize them under a single head. This is the highest stage that naturalism

[1] *Natural Religion*, London: Longmans Green & Co., 1889, 52.
[2] Ibid. pp. 17 f.

can reach, and it now breaks down under its inner contradictions, to make way for a higher form of religion, supranaturalism. This branches out in two directions, one monist and the other theist. The first, in India, repudiates naturalism negatively by reducing the world to illusion over against an absolute principle. The second, in Israel, repudiates it positively by enthroning an absolute personal God as its Creator and Lord. For monism, man must be his own saviour, for theism he is dependent on God.

The conclusion of the argument is not difficult to foresee. The final truth, which is at the same time, the absolute religion, will transcend this opposition, while preserving the truth in each type. Hartmann calls this 'concrete monism', which is the name he gives to his own philosophy. The Indian religions were abstract, surrendering the world and man to illusion so that man might find unity with God as the reality beyond this. The theistic religions left God over against man as person against person, so that the two could be related only through some form of mediation. One purchased unity with God by making it impossible to have a relation to him; the other established a relation by making unity impossible. We look for a coming world-religion that will avoid both mistakes, giving us at the same time a real relation and a genuine unity.

Such a religion does not need to be constructed *de novo*. If the Christianity of the churches and the creeds is far from it, it is present already in germ among the mystics. It derives from John rather than Paul; in it the Spirit is central and Christ himself is assimilated thereto. And the Spirit is both immanent and transcendent. All men participate in it, yet in none is it fully present. It is therefore transcendent enough for a religious relation to be possible, and immanent enough for that relation to be one of unity. The Spirit is the Atman of India and the God of the West. Such a religion will not recognize the distinction between man's faith and God's grace, man's reason and God's revelation. Nor will there be any distinction between man's suffering and God's, man's redemption and God's. For

F   81

the only God who can draw near to the human heart is a God who is unhappy, who suffers like him and like him needs redemption, but who at the same time bears an infinitely heavier burden of suffering than petty man does.[1]

The future lies, therefore, in a synthesis of East and West, but in this synthesis Christianity will be the senior partner. In his *Grundriss der Religionsphilosophie* Hartmann states this clearly. Schopenhauer made Indian religion absolute, as Hegel did Christianity. Both are mistaken. These represent two great streams of religious development, each of which has its own rights but the Christian stream has flowed onwards while the Indian has stagnated. Hence the next advance will come from the West rather than the East, with both indeed making their contributions to this, but with the Christian contribution the decisive one.[2]

[1] *Grundriss der ethischen Prinzipienlehre*, 1909, p. 216.
[2] *Grundriss der Religionsphilosophie*, 1909, p. x.

VII

The Turn of the Century

a. HISTORICAL RELATIVISM

THE beginning of the twentieth century marks a turning-point in the discussion we are following, and that for several reasons. In the first place, the results of historical criticism as applied to the New Testament equally with the Old had become common knowledge for the educated person, especially in Germany. In the second place, the horizon of such a person was now wider than ever before: his security even was threatened by a China in revolt and a modernized Japan. Thirdly, the East, thanks to the rise of modern universities in India and Japan, was producing interpreters of its ancient traditions schooled in Western techniques and using these for their apologetic. The world had undergone an unprecedented expansion and it was no longer clear that its centre remained in Europe. The assumption with which the West had hitherto operated, the assumption that civilization and history were the prerogative of the Mediterranean basin, was no longer tenable. Were our values not universal after all? Was our Christianity merely provincial?

To be sure, the new mentality was not entirely of recent growth. It was but the latest phase in that historical consciousness so distinctive of the nineteenth century. Was not one of its major triumphs the theory of evolution, for which even nature took on the features of historical process? Now the success of the historian was largely due to his suspension of moral judgment. He studied each episode in the past in the endeavour to learn just how and why it took the shape it did. The stranger such an episode, the greater the effort of research, interest, and sympathy required. His part was that of a spectator of events, surveying the past in an impartial and objective fashion. So doing, he found that much that at first seemed reprehensible was in fact appropriate to, perhaps necessary in, the situation out of which it arose. Hegel taught the European mind to think of everything in the past as relative, though at the same time as ministering to an absolute that could be found in the beliefs and institutions of nineteenth-century Europe. Once such an absolute came to be questioned, historiography led on to *Historismus*, a condition of things in which all standards of judgment disappear. Each complex of circumstances observed by the historian is a mere wave in the universal flux, no sooner visible than it begins to be merged under the next wave. From this standpoint our religion is historically conditioned like every other. The differences between religions lose their sharpness. Each has its share of truth and none may claim a monopoly. The most we can hope for is what is true *for us*.

It was with this problem that Eucken set himself to deal. The study of history does not terminate in frustration, though at a certain point it threatens to do so. What is needed is that we should carry our inquiry through to the end. When we do, we find that the historical process is more than a flux of events; there are islands in the stream, values that reveal themselves within the process while not in any sense its products. History shows us man claimed by that which transcends him. We can learn from the past only because there is a spiritual life in which we participate along with the men of the past. To be sure, on this view we shall cease to think of the eternal as bound up with a particular event in the past, and envisage it rather as offering itself to us in every moment of the temporal, though supremely disclosed in certain creative occasions.

From this it follows that there can be no such thing as an absolute religion, just because nothing within the temporal process can be absolute. What appears in the world is as such historically conditioned; it bears the stamp of the period at which it arose and will therefore never be more than partially adequate to the needs of other periods. The absolute religion is a reality, no doubt, but not a historical reality. It is to be found in, with, and under the historical religions, present in some to a higher degree than in others, but everywhere as alloy and nowhere as pure metal. So Eucken constructs what he calls 'characteristic religion' and allows to this the absolute status he denies to any of the historic creeds. It

appears, in so far as we understand it, not as the exclusive possession of a particular historical religion, but as the common aim and common fundamental energy of all religion. These historical religions are considered by us not as irreconcilable opponents, but as co-workers in the great enterprise of the spiritual redemption of humanity.

As certainly as there is one sole truth, there can be only one absolute religion, and this religion coincides entirely in no way with one of the historical religions.

The historical religions are not the truth itself, but appearances of the truth and pathways to the truth.[1]

It is therefore possible to classify religions and to grade them as higher and lower. Eucken argues for the superiority of Christianity, while allowing that the form in which it actually appears stands in need of revision. The criterion he applies is that of the power a religion possesses to foster and enhance the spiritual life. Here what is particularly important is its ability to master the obstacles to that life and to turn them into means of growth. In other words, we ask how each religion copes with the perennial problems of evil, pain, guilt, and death. Religions fall into two main groups, the religions of law and the religions of redemption. The second group divides into two sub-groups, comprising the Indian religions and Christianity respectively. India seeks redemption from the world, Christianity from a wrong condition in it. One bids us eradicate the will to live, the other offers a renewal of life by God's forgiveness. Christianity has shown us how to

---

[1] *The Truth of Religion*, London: Williams & Norgate, 1911, pp. 411, 535, 536.

make outward suffering a means to inward gain, it has brought God and man together whereas elsewhere they are separated. It excels, also, by its more positive attitude to the world and its broadly human character. It can be universalized as no other religion can.

The superiority of Christianity has thus been proved, at least to Eucken's satisfaction, but it is the superiority of an ideal or essential Christianity that differs markedly from what is found in the churches. Christianity is 'the highest embodiment of the absolute religion', 'the religion of religions', yet at the same time 'a fundamental revision of its traditional-existential form has become absolutely necessary'.[1] We are not concerned with the form this revision is to assume, but only with the question: If we are to abandon the claim that Christianity is absolute, can we then maintain that it is superior, that it is the highest of all known religions?

b. THE SUPERIORITY OF CHRISTIANITY

Troeltsch, in the earlier stages of his thought, was prepared to answer this question in the affirmative. Orthodoxy, he argues, set Christianity apart from all other religions as a supernatural irruption into history, attested by prophecy and miracle. This is no longer a tenable position, and Schleiermacher, Hegel, and Ritschl represent only so many vain attempts to resuscitate it. The only Christianity there has been, is, or ever will be, is one that is historically conditioned and therefore relative. The march of historical relativism may not be arrested at this point. Not that absolute values are surrendered. Troeltsch agrees with Eucken that they reveal themselves within history without being fully embodied therein. We can therefore continue to speak of an absolute religion only if we mean by this one that is located beyond history and is present within it merely as goal and ideal. But we need not for all that see in the history of religion only a welter of conflicting claims. We can reduce the number of

[1] *The Truth of Religion*, London: Williams & Norgate, 1911, p. 539.

religions that compete for allegiance today to three or four great types, perhaps to two, the monist and the monotheist. For the purposes of study we may be neutral as between these, but life requires us to choose, and choice needs a standard to direct it. Where then is this standard to be found?

Here Troeltsch follows Schleiermacher in assuming an 'essence' of religion common to all the religions, so that one among them will be the highest in which this common essence finds most adequate expression. But we shall not look for the essence in any principle of reason, nor shall we try to circumscribe it in any definition. It is present in the great religions as aim and endeavour. There is something they are all after, and in so far as we ourselves are religious persons we know from within the process what this is. Here we have the standard by which the truth in the various religions is to be measured, and it is an absolute standard. Our task is to identify the necessary in the conditioned, the eternal in the temporal.

The application of this standard takes place, not in any dispassionate study of the major spiritual alternatives that confront us, but as we participate in their living encounter. We must enter into alien forms of faith in the effort to understand them, their power over others, and what they have to offer us. The process is one of experience and what issues from it will be in the nature of personal conviction. This

has its objective ground in a careful survey of the relevant data, in unprejudiced appreciation of other forms of experience, and in conscientious weighing of the evidence; but in the last resort the decision remains subjective and personal, a matter of inner decision.[1]

From such a survey and comparison Christianity emerges as the highest of the religions known to us. It has effected the passage from nature to spirit more drastically than any other. 'Among the great religions Christianity is the strongest and most concentrated form of personal religiosity.'[2] We can confidently assert that

[1] *Die Absolutheit des Christentums*, 1912, pp. 66 f.   [2] Ibid. p. 86.

whatever is true in it will remain throughout the future. Should the worst happen and our civilization go down in ruin, its revival would bring with it a renewal of Christianity. Thus far may we go and we need go no farther. It is not necessary to maintain that no higher revelation can ever be vouchsafed to us, or that all men are one day to become Christians. Such desires are born of anxieties the genuinely religious spirit does not share. It is enough that we live by the truth given *to us*.

This conclusion, of course, rests on what Troeltsch calls 'the fine point of personal conviction'. Is there no train of reasoning that can fortify the conviction in question? Troeltsch thinks there is, and he finds it by comparing the different ways in which each religion claims to be absolute. For each religion makes a naïve claim to this effect, inasmuch as it offers itself as *the* way of salvation and not as one among several. When its adherents find that others also use the same language, they put forward for their own religion a reflective and sophisticated claim, advancing arguments to demonstrate its superiority. It then becomes possible to compare these arguments and therefore the claims that rest upon them. When we do so, we see reason to regard the Christian claim as better supported than the others. For here we have a religion that is universal and spiritual, with a succession of prophets culminating in Jesus, and authenticating itself by its power to reveal God and redeem men. In the last resort, the Christian gospel has its roots in the profound and mysterious relation of Jesus to God as Son to Father. In this, we may be sure, we have the highest that has yet been reached. As we follow Christ, we set our feet upon the path that leads, better than any other, to the absolute truth that transcends all the forms under which it is apprehended. Christianity

possesses the highest degree of validity among all the historical religions we are able to examine. We shall not wish to become Jews, nor Zoroastrians, nor Mohammedans, nor again Confucianists nor Buddhists. We shall rather strive continually to bring our Christianity into harmony with the changing conditions of life, and to bring its human and divine potentialities to the fullest possible fruition. It is the loftiest and most spiritual revelation of which we have any knowledge. It has the highest validity. Let that suffice.[1]

Such was Troeltsch's position when he wrote his *Die Absolutheit des Christentums* (1902).

c. SECOND THOUGHTS

Twenty years later, when Troeltsch came to take up again the theme developed in *Die Absolutheit des Christentums*, he decided that the treatment he had then given it needed to be modified at two important points. In the first place, he had come to rate the principle of individuality even more highly. Historical relativism was not to be combated as easily as he had once supposed. Perhaps even science and logic were as conditioned, as much the products of a particular civilization as its moral standards or its art-forms. Here we can detect the influence of Spengler upon him.

The universal law of history consists precisely in this, that the Divine Reason, or the Divine Life, within history, constantly manifests itself in always-new and always-peculiar individualisations—and hence that its tendency is not towards unity or universality at all, but rather towards the fulfilment of the highest potentialities of each separate department of life. It is this law which, beyond all else, makes it quite impossible to characterise Christianity as the reconciliation and goal of all the forces of history, or indeed to regard it as anything else than an historical individuality.[2]

In the second place, his further studies in Christian social ethics showed him that there is no such thing as Christianity *simpliciter*, but only a series of historically conditioned forms of that religion. The gulf between it and others had therefore begun to contract, and he came to see that, on grounds of personal conviction, their

---

[1] *Christian Thought*, University of London Press, 1923, p. 21.
[2] Ibid. p. 14.

adherents had as much right to judge *them* to be superior as he had to give Christianity this place.

For—and this is the point of supreme importance—the great religions have entered so deeply into the life and thought of those peoples with whom they are associated that the very standards with which the latter operate are derived therefrom. We find Christianity superior because it ascribes positive value to the world and history, stresses action, and sets a high value on the individual personality. But these are Western standards and they are largely Christian in origin.

Our European conceptions of personality and its eternal, divine right, and of progress towards a kingdom of the spirit and of God, our enormous capacity for expansion and for the interconnection of spiritual and temporal, our whole social order, our science, our art— all these rest, whether we know it or not, upon the basis of this deorientalised Christianity.[1]

We are guilty of the same fallacy as when we rate certain peoples as lower than ourselves in the scale of intelligence because they score badly in tests that assume familiarity with our urban civilization and its techniques. Behind us in Europe today lie centuries of interaction between secular and Christian ideals and forces. Our argument that Christianity is higher than other religions is nothing more than an assertion that our civilization is higher than others. There is nothing objective in such a judgment: it is the mere self-flattery of a provincial mind. We get out of the conclusion only what we put into the premises. An Indian may claim that Hinduism is superior with equal force, and with as little force, because he will employ a criterion that is largely the work of Hinduism. There is no neutral or impartial standpoint from which one can assess anything so all-pervading as a great religion. Do not suppose that it will help to ask an atheist for his opinion. If he is of the West, then, as the case of Nietsche shows, he will be a 'Christian atheist'. Of the religions therefore we must say that

---

[1] *Christian Thought*, University of London Press, 1923, pp. 24 f.

the question of their several relative values will never be capable of objective determination, since every proof thereof will presuppose the special characteristics of the civilisation in which it arises.[1]

Of Christianity we must be content to say:

It is God's countenance as revealed to us; it is the way in which, being what we are, we receive, and react to, the revelation of God. It is binding upon us, and it brings us deliverance. It is final and unconditional for us, because we have nothing else, and because in what we have we can recognise the accents of the divine voice.[2]

We may not therefore look for the triumph of one religion over the rest, but for fruitful co-operation between them. For it is clearly the will of God that others should see an aspect of his countenance that is hidden from us.

The great religions might indeed be described as crystallisations of the thought of great races, as these races are themselves crystallisations of the various biological and anthropological forms. There can be no conversion or transformation of one into the other, but only a measure of agreement and of mutual understanding.[3]

Thus historical relativism registers its triumph.

d. CATHOLIC COMMENT

Of the many criticisms of Troeltsch, the one that perhaps most deserves notice is Max Scheler's. The philosopher was then in his Catholic phase, and his Catholicism gave him a point of view from which Troeltsch's difficulties simply did not arise. He argues that neither positivism nor Protestantism can do justice to the question at issue. The former has a neat evolutionary scheme according to which the higher religions develop out of the lower, and the lower out of such primitive types of thinking as animism

---

[1] *Christian Thought*, University of London Press, 1923, p. 33.
[2] Ibid. p. 26.   [3] Ibid. p. 29 f.

and magic. In this enlightened century, we can dispense with any kind of religion, since in science we have a much more reliable guide! What is this, Scheler asks, but the stupid self-glorification of Western man, the bourgeois who imagines himself the climax of history? On the other hand, Protestant theology made the initial mistake of narrowing down God's dealing with the race to a single channel, and has actually denied any knowledge of him apart from Jesus Christ. Hence the effort of liberal theologians such as Troeltsch, embarrassed by the new knowledge the science of religion gives us, to save at least some scrap of 'absoluteness' for Christianity.

The Catholic is spared any such anxiety. For was he not taught to think of Plato and Aristotle as witnesses to the truth? The non-Christian religions may well contain within them germs of that which comes to fruition in Christianity. It is indeed one of the principles of the Church that truth is to be respected even where it is inadequately expressed or mixed with error. For example, when the Chinese revere Heaven, what they do is not lightly to be condemned. True, they worship as God what is really only his ordinance, the moral world-order he maintains. But is he not himself present in that? Granted the principle of a primitive revelation, it is possible to combine the finality of the Christian faith with a glad recognition of the relative truth of what falls outside this. All that is needed is to extend this approach to the wealth of material now at our disposal, and here anthropologists like Andrew Lang and P. W. Schmidt have shown us the way.[1]

A similar judgment is to be found in Von Hügel:

We religious men will have to develop, *as part of our religion*, a sense, not simply of the error and evil, but also of the truth and the good, in any and every man's religion. We will have to realise, with Cardinal John de Lugo, S.J. (who died in 1660), that the members of the various Christian sects, of the Jewish and Mohammedan communions, and of the non-Christian philosophies, who achieved and achieve their salvation, did and do so in general simply by God's grace aiding their

[1] *Vom Ewigen im Menschen*, 1933, pp. 716 ff.

good faith instinctively to concentrate itself upon, and to practise, those elements in the cultus and teaching of their respective sect, communion or philosophy, which are true and good and originally revealed by God. And, finally, we religious men, especially we Catholic Christians, will indeed never drop the noble truth and ideal of a universal unity of cultus and belief, of one single world-wide Church, but we will conceive this our deathless faith in religious unity as being solidly realisable only if we are able and glad to recognise the rudimentary, fragmentary, relative, paedagogic truth and worth in religions other than our own—a worth which, as regards at least Judaism and Hellenism, the Roman Church has never ceased to practise and proclaim.[1]

One can find equally liberal statements in the work of a devout historian like René Grousset. The Catholic does not need to make an exclusive claim for his faith. A certain natural knowledge of God, fragments of a primitive revelation, grace that comes to the help of every sincere seeker—these combine to enable him to recognize elements of truth in every religion that has won men's allegiance. It is not out of the question for him that this *preparatio evangelica* should include Confucius and Buddha as well as Plato and Aristotle. But there are distinct limits to this apparent liberalism. The truth in the non-Christian religions is expressly said to be 'rudimentary, fragmentary, relative, paedagogic' only. Scheler's criticism of Troeltsch therefore misses the point. It was because the latter saw so clearly that the non-Christian religions cannot be reduced in this way to mere handmaids of the Church that he raised the question how we, as Christians, are to regard them and how, in the light of what we know of them, we are to regard our own faith.

[1] *Essays and Addresses in the Philosophy of Religion*, London: J. M. Dent & Sons, 1921-26, i. 63.

VIII

Philosophy in East and West

THIS chapter and the next are meant to serve as connecting links between the historical portion of this study and the constructive section. Here I propose to consider how East and West differ in the presuppositions that govern everyday thought and action. Of course, one must bear in mind the complexity of both traditions. The East does not present us with a single point of view consistently developed. India and China are sometimes poles apart, with Japan as the exception that proves the rule. India has its six schools of philosophy, and we credit ancient China with three, the Confucian, the Legalist, and the Quietist. Again, two periods that are chronologically far apart may be psychologically and culturally akin. There are aspects of Indian thought that are alien to the modern Western mind but would have been appreciated at once by a man of the Middle Ages. Finally, the East equally with the West is in a state of turmoil; it is changing before our eyes, so that statements that were true ten years ago are now false. The most that anyone can make bold to offer is therefore a certain number of general contrasts, and even there we must bear in mind that what we see in another culture will not be identical with what those see who stand within it.

a. EXPERIENCE AND INTERPRETATION

I begin with F. S. C. Northrop's *Meeting of East and West*, confining myself to what in it is relevant to the present study. His thesis is that the East sets out from experience as immediate awareness, while the West is concerned to handle experience by conceptual interpretation, and that therefore each ought to learn from the other. It may be best to state this in his own words:

The Oriental portion of the world has concentrated its attention upon the nature of all things in their emotional and aesthetic, purely empirical and positivistic immediacy. It has tended to take as the sum total of the nature of things that totality of immediately apprehended fact which in this text has been termed the differentiated aesthetic continuum. Whereas the traditional West began with this continuum and still returns to local portions of it to confirm its syntactically formulated, postulationally prescribed theories of structures and objects, of which the items of the complex aesthetic continuum are mere correlates or signs, the East tends to concentrate its attention upon this differentiated aesthetic continuum in and for itself for its own sake.[1]

For immediate experience, we may say, the distinction between subject and object has not yet arisen; it is a continuous stream that carries along with it pains and pleasures, sensations of colour and sound, and so on. When attention is concentrated on the local here-and-now differences within the stream, we have the differentiated aesthetic continuum; when attention is withdrawn from these, we have the undifferentiated aesthetic continuum. But there is a third possibility. We may seek to order and manipulate experience by constructing concepts to group together a number of these local here-and-now differences and to forecast their future behaviour: we then check these generalizations by observation and retain or revise them as the evidence requires. The East operates the first two procedures, the West the third. Science is the *forte* of the latter, art and religion are the strong points of the former.

Some illustrations may help to bring out better what is meant. In Chinese art, the artist paints out of a sense of unity with nature; he must become one with bamboo or mountain before he sets brush to scroll. The Westerner paints objects that are immediately

[1] Op. cit. New York: Macmillan, 1946. p. 375.

apprehended, no doubt, but as signs of what conceptual thinking grasps, the Ideas. The Indian devotee empties his consciousness of the finite and transitory, that he may become one with the unchanging behind all change. The Western believer relates himself to a personal God who directs the detail of history according to a will man may hope to know. While the Oriental errs by yielding too easily to the circumstances of the moment, the sin of the Westerner is bigotry, fanatical adherence to general principles. The ethos of the East is detachment, that of the West attachment. 'Let go!' says one; 'Commit yourself!' cries the other. 'Not this! not that!' is the expression of the divine for the East, while the West speaks of God's character and purpose. Monotheism means for us a sharp separation between God and nature; the Hindu meets the one God in the forces of nature and even in images.

Paul Masson-Oursel confirms this analysis in his *Comparative Philosophy*.

All Asiatic logic, even when coloured with idealism, is concerned with things, substances or phenomena, and not with concepts. . . . As for ourselves, the East will teach us that our conceptual logic bears an exclusively European character.[1]

So where we say 'Socrates is mortal', the Indian would say 'There is a mortal man, Socrates'. He 'grasps the solidarity of two attributes of a single substance' where we relate two concepts.[2] Nor is it purely accidental that Socrates figures in the first sentence the Western student of logic is given. For it is he who more than any other gave our thought the direction it has followed ever since. The East had no Socrates.

In the East no man was found to distil from vulgar opinion and current language that basis of the logical spirit of the West—concepts; and it is impossible to exaggerate the importance of this fact.[3]

[1] Op. cit. London: Routledge & Kegan Paul, 1926, pp. 147 f.
[2] Ibid. p. 146.   [3] Ibid. p. 142.

If the difference between East and West lies in the fact that each emphasizes one of the two components of experience, reconciliation ought not to be difficult. Each party must learn to recognize that it has *a* truth, but that *the* truth is that which will unite both parties.

They can meet, not because they are saying the same thing, but because they are expressing different yet complementary things, both of which are required for an adequate conception of man's self and his universe. Each can move into the new comprehensive world of the future, proud of its past and preserving its self-respect. Each also needs the other.[1]

b. KNOWLEDGE AND WISDOM

Part of the value of the analysis in the previous section is that it illuminates some of those more obvious differences between East and West that by now have become part of the common consciousness with us. Thus, we know that the East is tolerant, the West intolerant, by tradition. China has its three religions, India accepts the superstition of the villager as *his* way to God as the philosopher's speculation is his; in Europe some of the most cruel wars were those waged over religion. Again, the East, we say is contemplative, static, conservative, while the West is active, dynamic, and progressive. As Keyserling puts it in more abstruse language, for the East 'significance is the primary, the eternal, and the truly real force' beside which the realm of appearance ranks only as so much illusion,[2] while for the West 'it is the mission of man to embody significance in appearance'.[3] This would mean, presumably, that the West is down-to-earth and practical as the East is not. Yet we must be wary of any such conclusion. What are we to make, in this connection, of the judgment that in the Orient

---

[1] *Meeting*, pp. 454 f.
[2] *Travel Diary of a Philosopher*, London: Jonathan Cape, 1925, p. 108.
[3] Ibid. p. 637.

all philosophy is ultimately for practical purposes, that ethics or the philosophy of life is the essential phase of philosophy, that the theoretical finds its sole justification in its service as a guide to the practical?[1]

A contemporary Indian thinker confirms this: 'In India, philosophy is sought for the sake of the one and only lesson it teaches man: how to attain and live the life in which is realized the all as himself and himself as the all.'[2]

The second quotation shows that the practical purpose is not at all a this-worldly one. Indeed, what is at stake here is just *what* is truly practical. The medieval Christian knew quite well that nothing mattered in comparison with the salvation of the soul. So the Indian even in his boldest flight of speculation seeks release and salvation from the illusion that is life in this world. The Taoist argues for quietism and a do-nothing policy because it is far more effective, more practical, in the long run than education, law, and morality. The practical aspect of Confucius and Moh Ti comes nearer to our feeling on the matter, though the ends sought by them are political and social rather than economic.

I would put it that the West seeks knowledge, the East wisdom. It is worth noting in this connection that, according to Masson-Oursel, while our philosophical tradition is divided between intellect and will, some giving the primacy to this and others to that, India and China have never recognized this distinction. The knowledge of the Upanishads is akin to that of the Old Testament, a knowledge that transforms and not merely informs. He adds that on this point Socrates stood where the East still stands. We ask how it was that he did not see that men sin by ill-will and not merely by ignorance. Perhaps he did not distinguish the two as we do. Perhaps what we thought was psychology pure and simple is *our* psychology and no more.

[1] *Philosophy East and West*, ed. Chas. A. Moore, Oxford University Press, 1944, p. 266.

[2] V. Subrahamanya Iyer in *Contemporary Indian Philosophy*, London: Allen & Unwin, 1936, p. 346.

Granted that the East seeks after wisdom, how does it suppose it attainable? Whereas the European wrestles with a problem in the hope of solving it, the Indian rather aspires to reach a new condition of consciousness.

The Westerner advances from thought to thought, inducing, deducing, differentiating, integrating; the Indian advances from condition to condition. The former rises higher and higher in the domain of abstraction, from particular to general concepts, from these to ideas, and so forth; the latter changes continually the form of his consciousness.[1]

This is so important that I add a quotation from Radhakrishnan:

Hindu systems of thought believe in the power of the human mind to lead us to all truth. Our ordinary mind is not the highest possible order of the human mind. It can rise to a level almost inconceivable to us. Each system prescribes a discipline or a practical way of reaching the higher consciousness.[2]

Even more striking is this from Aurobindo:

We mean by man mind imprisoned in a living body. But mind is not the highest possible power of consciousness; for mind is not in possession of Truth, but only its ignorant seeker. Beyond mind is a supramental or gnostic power of consciousness that is in eternal possession of Truth. This supermind is at its source the dynamic consciousness, in its nature at once and inseparably infinite wisdom and infinite will of the divine Knower and Creator. Supermind is superman; a gnostic supermanhood is the next distinct and triumphant evolutionary step to be reached by earthly nature.[3]

The presupposition of Indian thought is that consciousness functions at several levels. This explains how the belief in transmigration is possible, seems indeed the common-sense explanation

[1] *Travel Diary*, p. 258.
[2] S. Radhakrishnan in *Contemporary Indian Philosophy*, p. 266.
[3] Sisirkumar Mitra, *Sri Aurobindo and the New World*, 1957.

of the disparities life presents. It would be absurd to think of the rationalized consciousness of Western man as entering the world now as man, now as animal, and perhaps even as god. But here again we confront a different psychology from ours, and let us not forget that the Indian's psychology (what Jung would call 'metapsychology') is confirmed by his experience as ours is by ours. Consciousness, then, functions at a series of levels and at each it apprehends directly what is given. What appears to us fantastic speculation is sober report to him. His is a 'higher empiricism'.

That there is such a highest realm, to be reached as one carries thinking to the point where it transcends itself and becomes vision, some among us have maintained. In India, there is a recognized training, Yoga, for those who wish to reach the supraconsciousness and the truth it finds.

By heightening his power of concentration man gains possession of an instrument of immense power. If he controls this instrument perfectly it is possible for him to enter into direct contact with any object in the world, to act at a distance, to create like a god, to attain whatever he wishes. He has to direct his concentrated attention only towards one point, and he then knows everything concerning it. He need only turn to a problem to understand and solve it.[1]

Such is the insight given by the Tao.

> Without leaving his door
> He knows everything under heaven.
> Without looking out of his window
> He knows all the ways of heaven.
> For the further one travels
> The less one knows.
> Therefore the Sage arrives without going,
> Sees all without looking,
> Does nothing, yet achieves everything.[2]

[1] *Travel Diary*, pp. 263 f.
[2] Arthur Waley, *The Way and its Power*, London: Allen & Unwin, 1934, p. 200.

As has been noted in more than one quarter, there is something here that Bergson can help us to understand. Intellect, he tells us, serves the everyday purposes of life, and it does this by abstracting from the totality of life in order to manipulate it by means of concepts. As against this, philosophy should make use of intuition, which enables us to grasp life from within as a total movement. Thus, 'philosophy can only be an effort to dissolve again into the Whole'.[1] It might be an Indian speaking. But the *yogin* does not return to a condition prior to intellect, he advances through intellect to a country beyond it.

There is perhaps a closer relation between Indian thought and the existentialism of Jaspers and Marcel. For this, too, philosophy is an intellectual labour that leads to an extension and deepening of consciousness. One comes to the point at which the processes we call knowledge break down, to the limit-situations of guilt, pain, death, and so to the ultimate mystery that can be met only by the transformation of the self. What is found then can only be related in stammering fashion, perhaps better in a play than in a treatise. Or, when it is given the form of argument, the reader is constantly reminded that this is but a pointer to what does not admit of demonstration. But the existentialist must part company with the *yogin* at one point. There is no technique of the Transcendent in which one can be trained; the way thereto is by faith, hope, and the venture of one's whole self. 'What is so wonderful', says Keyserling, 'in Indian yoga

is the perfect rationality of its methods. We do, of course, not know whether it leads with certainty to the goal it is supposed to lead to, and whether the phenomena with which it is connected have been recognized and interpreted correctly; but in principle the possibility exists of testing the exactitude of its assertions along with its theories.'[2]

There are affinities also between the analytical psychology of Jung and Oriental thought, as he himself has often pointed out. The archetypes of the collective unconscious correspond to the

[1] *Creative Evolution*, 1911, p. 202.   [2] Op. cit. p. 560.

metaphysical realities of the supraconscious. In each case the way thereto is by a course of training and discipline under a master, and in each the motive of the quest is the desire for salvation.

Here, again, mutual understanding is called for. In East and West alike, we need both knowledge and wisdom.

c. ACCEPTANCE AND RENUNCIATION

In the popular judgment, one of the most important differences between East and West is that the former tends to renounce the world while the latter cheerfully and heartily accepts it. Two concepts in particular may be cited in support of this view, those of Maya and Nirvana. For does not the first mean that all things here below, ourselves included, are unreal, illusory, a mere play of Brahma, and as such not to be taken seriously? Contrast with this the Western emphasis on history as man's sphere of action and responsibility; he is here for a purpose, the world is for the making of his soul, and for what he does in it he will one day be called upon to render an account. Similarly, is not Nirvana a state of inaction, even perhaps of annihilation? At any rate, the desire for it is prompted by a sense of the worthlessness of the world as transitory and fraught with suffering. The West wants to change conditions, the East surrenders life as irremediable and seeks only to escape from it. Of course, it is clear that the East is here being understood in a restricted sense. The Confucian scholar shows no sign of judging the world an undesirable place, and the Zen devotee insists that *Samsara* is Nirvana, that here and now the Buddha-land is open to us to enter in. Only against India and, outside India, those who have accepted Buddhism, can this charge of world-rejection be brought.

Schweitzer tells us that he began his study of Indian thought because he was not convinced that this popular judgment, even supported by the authority of Schopenhauer and Deussen, was to be accepted without question. When he went to the sources, his doubts were strengthened. He came to the conclusion that the positive attitude to life was present in India from the beginning alongside the negative, and that the latter had no sooner established itself as negative than it had to face a counter-attack. Driven from one position to another, it is today on the point of being expelled entirely by the positive attitude to life. The Vedas show us a boisterous, hard-drinking warrior class as little disposed to renunciation as Homer's heroes. It was with the Brahmins that the ideal of renunciation originated and it was they who gave it a prestige that is only now being seriously shaken. Yet even the Brahmin had to allow that the ascetic should come to his rejection of the world through acceptance of it in the normal round of family and social life. Even Buddha linked his condemnation of the world as a place of suffering with a summons to self-perfection in thought, word, and deed, and also to compassion for all sentient beings. And the Gita preached *karmayoga* as a life of loving devotion amid one's daily duties in a spirit of inward detachment. But it was not till the nineteenth century and under the influence of the West that the claim was put forward that is now to be met with constantly, that Hinduism is only understood as resignation and flight from the world when it has first been misunderstood.[1]

In this last point Schweitzer is certainly correct. Whatever may have been the case in the past, the Hinduism of the future will regard social progress and social service as native to it, and not as a foreign import. The Ramakrishna Mission, Gandhi and Tagore are evidence enough.

Leave this chanting and singing and telling of beads! Whom dost thou worship in this lonely dark corner of a temple with doors all shut? Open thine eyes and see thy God is not before thee!

He is there where the tiller is tilling the hard ground and where the pathmaker is breaking stones. He is with them in sun and in shower, and His garment is covered with dust. Put off thy holy mantle and even like Him come down on the dusty soil![2]

[1] *Indian Thought and Its Development*, London: Hodder & Stoughton, 1936.

[2] Tagore, quoted in A. J. Appasamy, *Temple Bells*, London: S.C.M. Press, 1930, p. 126.

Even in the past, it is not clear that what are negativism and pessimism from our point of view were such for the Hindu and the Buddhist. A person may well count the world well lost for what is of so much more value than the world. It would seem that even those who, like Sankara, dismissed the world as illusion in fact accepted it as real for all practical purposes. The latter attitude is, of course definitely that of the Vaishnavite. While from the final standpoint this world is but an empty show, our life in it is not lived from this final standpoint, but from one that accepts it as the sphere of duty and achievement. And we in the West are supposed to be familiar with the question: 'What shall it profit a man, if he gain the whole world, and lose his own soul?' We too are bidden to look 'not at the things which are seen, but at the things which are not seen: for the things which are seen are temporal; but the things which are not seen are eternal'. In Buddhist countries such as Burma and Ceylon there is no less of the joy of life than there is in the West. That 'all life is suffering' no more militates against enjoyment than does the confession that we are 'miserable offenders'.

As the Middle Ages recognized that life must be lived on two levels, so did the East. The few are called to take the ultimate standpoint and deny the world, the many must live within it. And we need to bear in mind that the Oriental is not troubled by the urgency of our threescore and ten years. Salvation does not turn once for all on what we do here below. This life is important enough to be taken seriously, but it is not all the life we have. It is sufficient for most men if they use it as one step nearer to the goal. What is the meaning of obsession with the present moment where a succession of further opportunities is anticipated? Our categories of world-acceptance and world-denial do not admit of a simple application where this is the case.

There is, however, a real difference between the East and the West, and that in two respects. In the first place, they offer alternative solutions to the problem of how to close the gap between man's desires and the satisfactions open to him. We want more than life is willing to give us. Under the pressure of this state of things, the Occidental develops ever fresh means to the satisfaction of his desires. He speaks of a 'divine discontent'; need should become a spur to achievement, till the ideal condition is realized and all wants are met. Alas, he is never in fact satisfied. What is more serious is that he creates an economic system in which wants are stimulated by all sorts of means in order that goods may be produced and services afforded. The stimulation of desire has become a fine art with us, and we actually dare to hope that one day we shall have increased the wants of multitudes in Asia and Africa to the point at which—they will be happy? Oh, no, we shall be rich! The Oriental ideal, on the other hand, is reached by the reduction of one's desires to the level at which they can be satisfied. This ideal is embodied in the Confucian scholar, who asks only for a few books, wine, and the conversation of his fellow-scholars. But much less will do.

How admirable was Hui! With just a modicum of food and a gourd of water, and living in a mean alley-way: other men could not endure the misery of it, but Hui was not affected. He remained quite happy. Admirable indeed! [1]

Here again the Eastern standpoint is nearer to that of early and mediaeval Christianity than to our own. When an Indian official abandons office and power for the life of a *sannyasi*, the heart of his people responds. So did the heart of a mediaeval people when a monarch abdicated to enter a monastery.

In the second place, there are points both of agreement and of contrast in the *karmayoga* of the Gita and the 'inner-worldly asceticism' that Max Weber finds in Protestantism. In each case, a man is to discharge the duties laid upon him by society, and to do so in inward detachment, making of all that he does an offering to God. In each case, he hopes by this means to achieve salvation. But there are important differences. In India the ideal is embodied in the warrior and the householder rather than the merchant,

[1] E. R. Hughes, *Chinese Philosophy in Classical Times*, London: J. M. Dent & Sons, 1942, p. 30.

the duties are those required by tradition in accordance with the caste system, and there is none of that restlessness, that activity for its own sake, that makes for a mounting accumulation of capital.

In the West one acts primarily for the sake of the immediate result of the action, or because of love of activity as such, and this is not only the very opposite of *karmayoga*, but also perhaps, the secret of the West's bondage to the world and its values.[1]

[1] *Philosophy East and West*, p. 292.

IX

Christianity and Indian Religions

HUMANISM and the political religions apart, Christianity's only rivals for the spiritual allegiance of Western man are the religions of India. Here there are four possible attitudes that require to be considered. The first is *neutrality*, the attitude of the observer for whom both types of religion are valid and who, if choice is required of him, opts for the one that claims his attention at the moment. The second is *assimilation*, for which the differences between the religions are glossed over, and the two are reconciled by stating one in terms of the other. The third is *hostility*, when one is rejected outright in the name of the other. The fourth is *understanding*, when an attempt is made to appreciate the genius of each religion and to facilitate communication between them. I shall deal in the main with one representative of each attitude in the rest of this chapter.

a. NEUTRALITY

For the first I select Count Keyserling. From one point of view, his *Travel Diary of a Philosopher* is a masterpiece of what the Germans have taught us to call empathy, the ability to feel oneself into a standpoint and system originally alien. He tells us that he did not go abroad to extend his experience, but rather to show how a mind that is master of itself does but turn upon its own axis even while it circumnavigates the globe, because it enters into different forms of spiritual life, to find each appropriate and even inevitable in its own setting. Each style of life is understood and justified in its own place. In the East, therefore, Keyserling is critical of the West, but no sooner is he on American soil than the values of the West resume their hold over him. There is no over-all standard and the path to perfection is open within each culture. Perfection, that is, in a particular direction, though this will be compensated for by inadequacy elsewhere. 'Every appearance within its limits can give expression to Atman.'[1]

So in Ceylon the description of the world as *maya* becomes the only possible one amid such a riot of vegetation as surrounds him. That nothing is permanent, that life passes over into death and death into renewal of life—this is everyday experience in the tropics. One ceases to think, and something impersonal thinks in one. If then there is no permanent self, what room is there for any thought of immortality? One longs rather to be free, free for ever from the constriction of this luxuriant, entangling environment.

The introduction to India took place through a temple ceremony at Rameshvara in which he participated. Here he found an attitude to the world quite different from ours. To understand this, we must give up our assumption that there is a world that has been accurately described by Western science, and that those who think otherwise are merely foolish or ignorant. We need to recognize that world and consciousness are correlated or, to change the metaphor, that other peoples are receptive of wavelengths that escape us altogether.

Every form of consciousness reveals a different layer of nature. He who dwells in the world of the Hindu is subject to influences and has experiences unknown to others.[2]

Hence the Indian response to symbols is other than ours. He believes without 'believing that', as we cannot. He may commit himself to an avatar for salvation without supposing that such a being ever existed.

A meeting with a group of political exiles in Tsingtao won his sympathy for China.

[1] *Selbstdarstellung*, p. 15.   [2] *Travel Diary*, pp. 92 f.

All these statesmen take it as a matter of course that the organism of state rests on a moral basis, that politics are the external expression of ethics, and that justice is the normal emanation of good intentions; and it seems a matter of course to them, in quite a different sense from that in which the Sermon on the Mount does to the Christians: not as something which ought to be, but which happens only rarely, but as something which necessarily takes place.[1]

He caught a glimpse of Islam in India and felt himself at home. In a Moslem environment he became susceptible to the values of monotheism, the dignity it confers on those who know themselves to be in immediate relation to God, especially when this is fortified by belief in predestination, so that one is secure in the hands of God and called to serve him. Islam is a soldier's religion, and it breeds greatness of soul, self-confidence, and readiness to accept the fellow-believer as a brother, since all human distinctions vanish with God.

All this is interesting and much is of value. Yet no clear conclusion emerges. In Japan, Keyserling finds Mahayana superior to Christianity; in America he reverses the relation. Indeed, the weakest part of the book is the final section, in which he looks back on his travels from an American perspective and finds in favour of the West. It is now to be praised for its activism, and even the missionary, previously condemned as an intruder upon a higher culture, is now justified. For is he not the bearer of 'a gospel of creative work and action?'[2] Further, the West has what Hegel termed 'objective spirit': the good is not left to individuals to will, but is built into institutions. Men do the right because it is expected of them, because it will be reciprocated, because their advantage points in that direction. Nor is this mere utilitarianism. It has educative value and may awaken spontaneity, so that a man comes to do of his own accord what society expects of him.

Whereas in our case even the man who is inwardly coarse is forced, to a certain extent, to act according to the highest ideals, nothing

---

[1] *Travel Diary*, p. 382.   [2] Ibid. p. 604.

compels the Asiatic to appear cultured where he is not, and for this reason the behaviour in practice of the average man in the East leaves more to be desired than that of the same class in the West. On the whole, we act better than we are.[1]

A dubious advantage indeed!

b. ASSIMILATION

One reaction to the discovery of India's rich spiritual heritage was an unwillingness to admit that it might be basically different from our own tradition. The conflict of truths is not easy to accept, and we prefer to take refuge in something like the 'perennial philosophy' that Aldous Huxley constructs. This assimilates Christianity to Indian thought till it virtually loses everything distinctive of it. The reconciliation of religions is achieved by the surrender of one party to the dispute. What happens is that all representatives of Christianity are dismissed unheard except the one whose agreement to such an arrangement is guaranteed in advance—the mystic. So when Huxley states the 'four fundamental doctrines' that are 'at the core of the Perennial Philosophy', he cites Suso and Eckhart for Christianity and the Sufis for Islam. Now, there is no doubt that mysticism is one the world over, but what is entirely overlooked in this argument is that mysticism as a system of practice and thought is central for India, marginal for Christianity. Heiler's distinction between the mystical and the prophetic types of piety may need qualification, but it is a valid protest against the hasty assimilation of what are really quite diverse spiritual types. And it is not clear that the three great monotheist religions would agree to be described in terms of a philosophy, even a perennial one.

How unjustified and unsatisfactory such a procedure is may be seen from W. T. Stace's *Time and Eternity* (1952). To be sure, he anticipates criticism by denying that he merely takes Indian thought as his starting-point; he does but set out the common

[1] *Travel Diary*, p. 595.

elements in the various faiths. But we have only to look at his description of religion to see that it does not apply to Christianity as usually understood.

Religion is the desire to break away from being and existence altogether, to get beyond existence into that nothingness where the great light is. It is the desire to be utterly free from the fetters of being. For every being is a fetter. Existence is a fetter. To be is to be tied to what you are. Religion is the hunger for the non-being which yet is.[1]

What has this in common with the Sermon on the Mount or Wesley's hymns? Nothing whatever. So when he looks for evidence to support his thesis, Stace goes to the mystics and not to the New Testament. Eckhart, Sankara, and the Sufi devotees bear witness to a common vision. Undoubtedly, but Eckhart stands outside the main Christian tradition while Sankara is one of the makers of the Indian tradition.

Stace further distinguishes between the negative and the positive divine, and asserts that their claims are equal. From the first standpoint God is 'not this, not that', 'the nameless nothing', 'the non-being that also is', and so on. For the second he is personality, justice, love. The whole treatment is heavily biased in favour of the first approach, and the Indian scriptures and the Christian mystics are quoted in its support. On the positive divine we have only a few general statements, and those gravely qualified. We are told what we predicate of God differs in kind, and not merely in degree, from the same thing predicated of man. This means

that there is no comparison between God's love and ours, that his love, and he himself, belong to a wholly different order from that in which we, in our natural moments in the time-order, live and move.[2]

This may be good Vedanta, it is certainly not Christianity.

[1] Op. cit. p. 5.   [2] Ibid. p. 155.

Stace frankly admits that the negative divine has no place in the Gospels, but urges that Christ's mission was to teach what 'the plain man' needed rather than to provide material for philosophers and theologians. A patronizing attitude indeed!

c. HOSTILITY

We have already had a notable instance of hostility, the preference of Indian religion to Christianity, in Schopenhauer, and this reappears in Nietzsche. Though he finds neither religion satisfactory when judged by his standard of the will-to-power, Buddhism is reckoned superior to Christianity, since it bids man rely on himself and not look for supernatural assistance. His own doctrine of the eternal recurrence is of the same order. It is the utter rejection of any purpose of the universe, and as such it is 'the European form of Buddhism' to which science is inexorably leading us.[1]

Leopold Ziegler builds upon Nietzsche, but supports his thesis with a much greater weight of argument. He tells us that Neumann's translation of the Pali scriptures came to him with the force of a revelation. It convinced him that Buddha was no pessimist or quietist; on this point, the Western interpretation was wrong. Henceforth, there must be no 'Monroe doctrine' to forbid the Western soul to open itself to what the East has to give. True, we can never be Buddhists. But our greatest need today is for a new religion. And since science has destroyed for us all possibility of belief in God, it must be a religion without God. To this who can help us better than Buddha?

According to Ziegler, one of the outstanding phenomena of modern times is the rejection of God combined with the retention of religion. Fichte, Shelley, Feuerbach, and Nietzsche are instances of this new attitude. Yet it is not as new as we think. For it was anticipated by Nicolas of Cusa and his *docta ignorantia*. He struck the deathblow at all attempts, from Anselm onwards, to 'demonstrate God's existence', i.e. to show from the objects in the world

[1] *Will to Power*, London: Allen & Unwin, 1909, i. 50.

that there is a superior object that is necessary, that is such that no greater object can be conceived, and so on. For Nicolas God is not the most eminent of all objects; he is beyond definition and description, beyond language even. He may neither be imagined nor thought. He transcends Being and Non-being alike. The good cardinal did not see whither he was travelling, but we can. The God he reaches by this road is the God whom the 'godless' acclaim. He is the Brahma of the Upanishads and the Nirvana of the Buddhists.

God must go, but religion must remain. Man cannot live without it. And Gautama has shown that God is not necessary to a religion by which a civilization is sustained and in which multitudes find support for daily life.[1]

In *Der ewige Buddho* (1922) this religion without God is presented as the logical development of Protestantism, the latter being itself only one form of something much older and more fundamental. 'Protestantism arises wherever the act that saves man and the world is the responsibility of man himself, man in this world of time and space.'[2] Shades of Martin Luther! Hence Buddha is the supreme Protestant. And Nietzsche is saluted as the Buddha both of this age and the coming one. It is only regretted that the vehemence of his attack on Christianity galvanized it into a final spasm of effort just as it was about to fall dead.

Where Ziegler differs from Nietzsche is in his estimate of the will-to-power. The defeat of Germany in the 1914-18 war taught us that the cult of power is deathly. But he ascribes the disaster that has befallen Europe, not to its abandonment of Christianity, but to the Christian influence at work in its history. Whereas Buddha repudiated a permanent self, Jesus put this in the centre of his teaching. Hence he must be held responsible for the self-assertion that has been the curse of Christendom. 'Power is the sole and final virtue of the European Christian; in it alone does he really believe; to it he prays and to it he sacrifices.'[3] We measure life by its power to produce and then fall victims to

---

[1] *Selbstdarstellung*, 1923; *Gestaltwandel der Götter*, 1922.
[2] Op. cit. p. 58.   [3] Ibid. p. 382.

what we have produced. Not that the Christian centuries were wholly in error. But they passed over the one thing needful. Gautama knows nothing of this imperious self; he does not cut up the world into fragments that he may bind these together again by means of laws. Whereas for us the individual self is the threshold everything must cross if it is to become real to us, he would have us lower this threshold till it approximates to zero, when a whole new and liberating experience will be ours. His saving formula runs: 'That does not belong to me.' We are to reject the Western notion that the world is there for us to possess it.

Yet activism is not to be disposed of so easily, and in the end light breaks for Ziegler in the West and not in the East. For man's vocation is to create 'God'. By this word we can nowadays mean only an idea, the kind of idea of which the psychologists say that it is a force for action. God is the point of unity towards which the world aspires, the reconciliation of those powers and purposes that would otherwise be in conflict. God is 'not this, not that', not Zeus, not Brahma, not Christ, not anything that may be known or named. God is not 'a thing in itself', but 'a thing to itself', an impulse in man towards its own realization. God is a tendency that awaits from man the decision whether it will reach or miss its goal. Man effects his salvation by producing his saviour!

d. UNDERSTANDING

Since understanding will be my concern in all that follows, I shall content myself here with a brief reference to A. N. Whitehead. For him, Buddhism and Christianity are 'the two Catholic religions of civilization' and

if we have regard to clarity of idea, generality of thought, moral respectability, survival power, and width of extension over the world, then for their combination of all these qualities these two religions stand out beyond their competitors.[1]

[1] *Religion in the Making*, Cambridge University Press, 1926, p. 44.

For a judgment on their respective worth, Whitehead operates with two criteria, their treatment of the problem of evil and their conception of God. On the first point, Christianity is 'a religion seeking a metaphysic' and Buddhism 'a metaphysic generating a religion'.[1] Or, in the language with which Marcel has made us familiar, Buddhism offers a solution of the problem of evil, while Christianity sees in it a mystery with which we can learn to live victoriously. The latter is accordingly 'less clear in its metaphysical ideas, but more inclusive of the facts'. How pain came about it cannot say; indeed, it directs attention to the evil we do rather than to that which we suffer. It certainly does not accept the thesis that 'all life is suffering'. But it offers us 'the religious fact' of Christ and in him a vision of how God is ever engaged in transmuting evil into good by taking it up into himself.

What now of the second point, the conception of God? Whitehead thinks that here Christianity is handicapped by its Hebrew heritage. It has taken over the transcendent, intensely personal, and terrifying God of the Old Testament. The peoples of the Far East have another conception of the divine as either an impersonal world-order or the reality of which the world is but an appearance. The merit of Christianity is that, while adopting the Semitic concept, it has not been confined to it. This is especially due to the Fourth Evangelist, whose Logos-doctrine qualifies transcendence by recognizing immanence.

So these two great religions confront each other, and confront also that new phenomenon, science. They do not find it easy to understand each other. They differ in their conceptions of God and of the ultimate fate of the soul. In their moral codes they largely agree; yet even here Christianity aims at the fulfilment of personal life, while Buddhism bids us overcome, not merely selfishness, but even, it would seem, selfhood as such. Again, each religion has its saviour. But Buddha and Christ are not saviours in the same sense. One brought a doctrine, the other gave his life. There is therefore opposition and not merely

[1] *Religion in the Making*, Cambridge University Press, 1926, p. 50.

difference. Is this condition to continue? Whitehead pleads that it should not. In the past 'each religion has unduly sheltered itself from the other'; let them now look 'to each other for deeper meanings'.[1]

Whitehead's treatment of our problem is slight in comparison with the others considered in this chapter. That was necessarily the case, as it is but part of a much larger study. But it has one great advantage over the others. It is not superficial. As such, it is much more worthy of consideration. So that, if the reader is disposed to travel farther with me along this road, this is the direction in which we shall proceed.

[1] *Religion in the Making*, Cambridge University Press, 1926, p. 146.

X

Criticism

a. METHOD

BEFORE continuing the journey, it may be as well to look back upon the road hitherto traversed. We have seen how the problem of the relation between Christianity on the one hand and Islam and the Oriental religions on the other emerged in the thirteenth century. We have noted certain solutions of this problem that have shown themselves to be open to criticism, and the time has now come to consider these in greater detail. They are five in number:

1. Christianity stands over against its rivals as truth against error.

2. The other religions contain an admixture of truth and error, perhaps because they draw upon a primitive revelation since largely obscured. Christianity can therefore recognize in them a preparation for the Gospel; it comes not to destroy, but to fulfil. It accepts and completes the truth that was present elsewhere in fragmentary fashion.

3. Christianity is the absolute religion, the culmination of a process of development in which the other religions are moments, each justified in its place but each transcended in its turn.

4. There is no absolute religion, but Christianity is the highest. It is superior to all rivals.

5. No comparison is possible between religions, since each is a whole that carries its own standards within itself. Each embodies the form of spiritual life appropriate to a particular culture. Christianity is 'God's countenance as revealed to us'.

These are the possible solutions now to be considered. But first something will need to be said on the standpoint from which this enquiry is conducted. The standpoint is not that of theology, but that of the philosophy of religion. The theologian's approach to the subject-matter of this study has been stated quite clearly by Tillich:

It should elaborate the motives and types of religious expression, showing how they follow from the nature of the religious concern and therefore necessarily appear in all religions, including Christianity in so far as it is a religion. A theological history of religion also should point out demonic distortions and new tendencies in the religions of the world, pointing to the Christian solution and preparing the way for the acceptance of the Christian message by the adherents of non-Christian religions. One could say that a theological history of religion should be carried through in the light of the missionary principle that the New Being in Jesus as the Christ is the answer to the question asked implicitly and explicitly by the religions of mankind.[1]

I need not consider here the justification for, or the value of, such an enquiry. Suffice it to say that my own purpose is very different. It is neither apologetic nor missionary. The finality of Christianity is not the initial assumption. It is one of the questions to be answered in the course of the enquiry. While the approach is from a Christian standpoint, the Christian allegiance of the writer is, as it were, held in solution throughout. It is liable to revision at any moment as the argument may require. There is no claim therefore to impartiality; that is probably not possible and perhaps not desirable. But it is hoped that the presuppositions with which one operates will be brought out into the open and checked against the evidence from time to time.

But what exactly is meant by one's 'Christian standpoint' and 'Christian allegiance'? For, as the preceding discussion will by now have made plain, the conclusion at which one arrives in this matter is largely decided in advance by the conception one has of

[1] *Systematic Theology*, London: Nisbet & Co., 1953, i. 44.

Christianity. In the relation between Christianity and the Eastern religions, the first term is more variable than the second. For while the second can be fixed by scholarship with some degree of accuracy, personal conviction enters into the determination of the first. Here again it is necessary to bring to light the assumptions with which one operates.

As I see it, the Christian is under two obligations in this matter, one to truth and one to love, and these have equal claim upon him. On the one hand, he must stand by that which convinces him of his truth. Not, to be sure, that he will do so with a closed mind. Rather will he hazard this truth continually afresh by exposing it to all the winds that blow and retain it only because it roots itself the more firmly as a result. On the other hand, he will look with charity, as on all men, so on all manifestations of the spiritual life. He will therefore approach with respect and reverence the religions that have guided men for centuries and continue to do so to this day. He will put on them the best possible interpretation and will be willing to enter into a relation with them in which he will receive as well as give. The precept of neighbour-love may not be restricted to individuals, it must be extended to the faiths that the Christian is tempted to regard as rivals, but with which he needs to acknowledge himself akin.

Nor is this relation between truth and love one of tension. The claim of truth includes within it that of love. Here, to be sure, we have to choose between the two interpretations of Christianity that have been current since the beginning, one exclusive and the other inclusive. For the first, the revelation of God in Christ is confined to a single stream of history, that which rises in Israel. For the second, what is revealed in Israel and in Christ is a dealing of God in mercy with all men at all times. The crucial significance of Christ is maintained on either view, but in the second case he is the point at which God so discloses himself that it can be seen that he is present at every point. For myself, the inclusive interpretation is the only possible one. The problem that has exercised so many good Christians, the problem of the multitudes who have died without hearing of

Christ and of those who died before he came, arises out of a failure to grasp the import of his revelation. The God who has come to us in him may not be restricted to him. Indeed, did he not come thus that he might open our eyes to see that none is without him?

In other words, my sympathies are with Sebastian Franck and Schelling, for whom Christ is 'the light that lighteneth every man that cometh into the world'. He is at once historical and universal, because in Jesus of Nazareth there came to its fullest expression that presence of God that is with every man, or rather, that presence of God in virtue of which he is constituted man. As such he is at once manifest in a community that acknowledges him as Lord and latent as an influence that is at work even where he is unknown or actually denied. Neither of these forms exhausts his fullness, for each has something that the other lacks. If the manifest Christ is served by truth, the latent Christ sets no bounds to love.

b. TRUTH AND ERROR

So much for the question of method. We may now address ourselves to the first of the five solutions to our problem enumerated above. For this, all religions are false save one's own and this alone is true. It might seem not worth the trouble to criticize this, for it can surely not now be held by anyone who has some knowledge of the great religions of the East. As we saw, it was soon found necessary to modify this claim on behalf of Christianity. The Moslem devotee and the Chinese scholar forced upon the missionary some degree of recognition. Yet it would be a mistake to dismiss this naïve view without further consideration, and that for two reasons. In the first place, we need to appreciate the measure of justification it originally had. The Hebrew prophet, faced with the licence of Baal-worship, the magic practices of Babylon, and the superstitions of the Hellenistic world, swept them away as false and called men to acknowledge the one true God. The missionaries who brought the Gospel to our forefathers felt in much the same way. They might, with Gregory the Great, be ready to facilitate the transition from the heathen temple to the Christian Church, but idolatry was abhorrent. Islam shocked the mind of Christendom; it seemed a devil's parody of the faith, and as such to be rejected with horror. When the categories of truth and error were first employed in this connection, they must have seemed the only possible ones.

In the second place, we should not overlook the element of truth in this naïve view. It is right in its insistence that the distinction between truth and error is as valid in religion as elsewhere in human experience. The mistake lies in supposing, first, that the true and the false in religion are to be identified with particular religions, and, second, that in the case of the true the identification is with one's own religion. We should rather think of truth and error as present in all religions, for are they not all historical phenomena, man's endeavour to come to terms with the Transcendent? They are true in so far as they apprehend the Transcendent aright, false in so far as they fail to do so. Since truth *is*, we are called to be resolute in its service; since it is never in our possession but always beyond us, we are to serve it without fanaticism, biogotry, or intolerance. It is a false charity that regards everything that is religious as therefore good. The charge that many Indians bring against the Biblical religions, the charge of exclusiveness, is justified where they claim a monopoly of the truth, not justified where they assert that the distinction between truth and falsehood is a vital one.

This brings us to the final solution we saw reason to question. I do not see how it is possible to place all religions on the same level, to assert that they are equally true. This is a view that has considerable support in the West today as well as in the East, and it is not without justification. It came as a surprise to many Europeans to find in the Islamic countries how religion permeates all life, how India and Japan have known for centuries of faith and love on man's part and grace on God's. The Christian who hears for the first time of Asoka notes with shame the contrast with his own imperial patron, Constantine. The discovery of a world of spirituality hitherto unknown forced on the West the surrender of its self-satisfaction and arrogance. Once we had abandoned our own position of superiority, we seemed to be on a plain, with everything on the same level.

Granted that we can see how such an opinion came to be entertained, it does not follow that it is plausible. One does not need to bring one's own religion into the picture. Is it really possible to maintain that there is no significant distinction between the worship of the synagogue and the practices of Tibetan lamaism? Or that Mohammed is on the same moral level as Buddha? We are back at the insistence that truth and error are as sharply opposed in religion as elsewhere.

Again, is it only a debating point that those who maintain that all religions are equally true invariably go on to assert that certain religions are in grave error because they do not recognize this, and that they ought to abandon this mistaken position for the true one? It is assumed, at times even claimed, that the religions that acknowledge all to be on the same level are *ipso facto* on a higher level than the others!

Again, if all religions are equally true, on what grounds does one follow this rather than that? Presumably the question is answered for one by the accident of birth. I believe in the religion into which I was born and in which I was brought up. But this seems to me destructive of the nature of religious conviction. I must begin, to be sure, by appropriating at second-hand the content of the tradition in which I stand; but I must go on to make it my own. We are not satisfied that a man should be a Conservative merely because he was born into a household that had always voted in that way; he ought to have convictions of his own. So in religion a man should come to the point at which he lives at his own charges: brought up a Christian, he chooses whether he will remain such or cease from that allegiance. In either case, he throws in his lot with truth as he sees it and rejects error.

c. CHRISTIANITY AS FULFILMENT

Is it possible to regard the non-Christian religions generally as one can regard Israel and classical antiquity, as a preparation for the Gospel? They are, on this view, so many aspirations to that which they cannot of themselves attain, so many expressions of a need only to be met in Christ. He comes to them, therefore, not to destroy but to fulfil. The Hindu or the Buddhist ought then to feel that in becoming a Christian he has lost nothing but has gained much, and that in particular all that was true in his old allegiance has been preserved in the new and indeed enhanced therein. There is something attractive about this view, and we have met it in the Protestant Schleiermacher and the Catholic Scheler. The day will come, says the former, when 'all religions will be visible in Christianity'. In the latter, this view receives additional support in the appeal to a primal revelation, an original disclosure of God to which all branches of the human race have fallen heir. It will be necessary therefore to glance briefly at this suggestion.

The existence of 'high gods of low races' cannot be questioned. In Ghana I was told that the ordinary man fully recognizes a supreme God who is Creator and Lord of all, though his prayers are directed not to him, but to some one of a whole host of minor spirits. As it was put to me: 'When you have a request to make to a chief, you do not think of going direct to him; you approach him through one of his subordinates.' In China Heaven plays a similar rôle, and in country districts I have heard reference made to 'the Heavenly Grandfather'. But there are other explanations of this phenomenon than a primitive revelation. Indeed, the theory of such a revelation must be regarded as a myth, that is, as the presentation in the language of history of that which does not belong to history but makes it possible. As such, it has its value. For it can be interpreted as referring, not to something that took place in the remote past, but to something that underlies every moment in the present. In other words, we might more legitimately speak of a basic revelation, that dealing of God with

man in virtue of which he is man, a being to whom God speaks
and who makes answer to him in acceptance or rejection.

From this digression we return to the theme of fulfilment.
It is contended that Christianity takes upon itself, includes, all
that is true, let us say, in Hinduism. But there is an obvious
source of error here. The Christian is only entitled to claim that
the Gospel does justice to the truth *he* finds in Hinduism. What
has to be shown rather is that it can do justice to the truth the
devout Hindu finds there. However convinced the Christian
may be that the hope of Israel became actuality in Christ, there
are Jews who have read the Gospels and come to revere the
figure portrayed in them who yet find that in their Jewish
heritage which is lacking in Christianity. Synesius could accept
Christianity as preserving what he valued. Symmachus could not.
What is possible is the judgment of the convert that he has lost
nothing but gained much by a change of allegiance. This is
something that is true for him personally, and as such is beyond
dispute. But equally beyond dispute is the judgment of his
neighbour that such a change would mean an impoverishment
not to be contemplated. For our purpose, the evidence is
indecisive.

When therefore Martin Wight says, in criticism of Arnold
Toynbee, that the higher religions 'forfeit their historical significance except in so far as they are related to Christianity',[1] he goes
much too far. For this judgment is put forward as that of a
professional historian who is also a Christian. It is for me out of
the question that spiritual structures of the value and power of
Hinduism, Buddhism, and Islam should be dismissed so lightly.
The great religions are to be accepted for their own sake and not
for the tribute they pay to our religion. What they say to us is
not decisive for their worth, but what they have said to the
multitudes who found shelter and inspiration in them. I could not
agree that even the religion of Israel is without independent
historical significance, and much less would this be the case with
those religions that spoke to other civilizations than our own.

[1] In *A Study of History*, Oxford University Press, vii. 748.

One further point. This claim to fulfil might be put forward on behalf of other religions. This is in fact taking place. For the Jew, Christianity and Islam are the means by which God leads the Gentiles out of heathenism towards the pure monotheism for which they are not yet ready. The Moslem acclaims Mohammed as the bearer of the final revelation for whom Moses and Jesus prepared the way. The most distinguished Buddhist leader in modern China was wont to say that Buddhism could find a home for everything in Christianity except the belief in a personal God. That error once discarded, the rest was truth that could be preserved. An Indian may confidently hold that, precisely because of its inclusive character, Hinduism can give hospitality to whatever truth other religions contain. The claim that a religion fulfils all religions is clearly the expression, on the plane of historical judgment, on one's personal attachment to that religion.

d. CHRISTIANITY AS ABSOLUTE

I come now to Hegel's grandiose demonstration of the history of religion as at the same time a logical development culminating in Christianity as the absolute religion? What is to be said of this? It is now agreed that the scheme, imposing though it is, is imposing only because it sacrifices history to logic. The facts themselves go into the witness-box against Hegel. There is no evidence whatsoever of any necessary development in religion, of any process by which it advances from stage to stage to come to itself finally in one particular religion. The history of religion shares the features common to all history. It is a record, not of steady progress, but of advance and retreat, of brilliant achievement and shameful failure. The Christian will see in it also the record of God's disclosure and man's response thereto, sometimes in acceptance and sometimes, alas, in rejection. It knows tragic loss, as when so great a prophet as Zoroaster left so little behind him; isolation, as in the case of Chinese thought; and calamitous misunderstanding, as when Christianity failed to give Mohammed what he needed, or he could not find it there. It knows also the conflict of values, when one apprehension of God is countered by another, equally sincere, but incompatible with it.

A more adequate analogy than the logical would be the biological. Biological evolution tells the same story of effort often wasted, possibilities thwarted, and tracks that seem to lead nowhere. If Bergson is right, man is not the crown of creation in the sense that all led up to him. There are other lines of development, at least one of which leads to a type of life that has preserved powers lacking in man. We may not say that the social instinct of the bee was a means to man's intelligence; it is of a different order and has a value of its own. So Confucius and Buddha claim attention in their own right and not merely for the service they can render to Christianity.

The assertion that any religion is absolute encounters at the outset two major difficulties. In the first place, one needs to know for which form of the religion the claim is made. Christianity exists in a rich diversity of forms, between which there is rivalry and at times even open opposition. We smile at Hegel's identification of the absolute religion with Lutheranism in his own peculiar interpretation of it. But is not the claim that any of us makes for Christianity necessarily in the name of Christianity as he himself understands it? And how can this be distinguished in the long run from attaching an absolute value to our own opinions? True, the attempt is made in certain quarters to avoid so unfortunate a conclusion by distinguishing between 'empirical Christianity', which can be surrendered to the relativity of all human things, and Christianity as revelation, which is independent of our judgment. But is it? Is not this second form of Christianity simply Christianity in the form that commends itself to those who employ this argument? It is another version of empirical Christianity and not anything of a higher order.

Consider, for example, this criticism of Troeltsch:

We speak familiarly of the Christianity of the Apostolic Age, of the Middle Ages, of the Reformation, of the twentieth century, meaning by these general phrases the total positive reaction to Christ in different epochs. That this reaction, whatever age be taken, has been profoundly imperfect and in that sense wholly relative, no reasonable person, it may be presumed, could be tempted for a moment to deny. . . . But when serious thinkers raise the question whether Christianity is or is not final and absolute, the real issue is, or ought to be, a very different one. Now we are dealing with 'Christianity' in quite another sense. Now it stands not for the reaction of man but for the action of God— for the revelation of God's holy love in Christ, for all that is meant by the Incarnation, the Atonement, the Resurrection, for the great things which the Father has promised or accomplished in the Son for us men and our salvation, for all that God is offering to the world in his declared Gospel. And to affirm the absolute and final character of Christianity in *this* sense merely proves that we understand what Christianity means.[1]

But is this to use the term 'Christianity' 'in quite another sense'? I fail to see this. Professor Mackintosh is merely asserting that Christianity as he and certain others understand it is absolute. What he describes is definitely not 'the action of God' but 'the reaction of man' thereto, a set of doctrines, each of them capable of many interpretations, by which men have sought to express what they found in Christ. The same writer goes on to say that

the finality of Christ and what he imparts can justly be called in question only when a loftier fact than holy love has come into view— then, but not till then.

But is not this the fallacy pointed out by Troeltsch, the fallacy of supposing one has demonstrated Christianity to be absolute or superior when one has assumed as much at the outset by taking a Christian standard as absolute or superior?

So much for the difficulty that arises from the fact that those who claim that Christianity is absolute confine that claim to one form of it—that which they themselves hold—while rejecting it

[1] H. R. Mackintosh, *Types of Modern Theology*, London: Nisbet & Co., 1937, p. 215.

for others. The second difficulty is that a religion is a historical phenomenon, arising at a particular point within history and a particular society, and as such conditioned and relative. That indeed, is essential to its success. That which was, as it were, in the air, not committed to any specific human situation, would meet no one's needs and would pass away, leaving no trace behind it. The message of the Hebrew prophets was for their own small kingdom in peril from the world-powers of the day, the Cross and Resurrection of Jesus are intimately related to the hopes and fears of Israel, the Pauline message was for the urban populations of the Mediterranean world in the first century, and so on. And a religion must pay what Hocking has called 'the price of existence'; if it is exactly suited to one period or people, it must be re-thought and re-stated if it is to commend itself equally to others. Nothing in this world of space and time is absolute. Only God himself is. An absolute religion is a contradiction in terms. If this is so, a serious question confronts us. It was said earlier that religion requires an absolute, since without this man cannot live. Where is such to be found?

e. RELATIVISM AND FAITH

We can no longer postpone a reckoning with historical relativism. How can we reconcile the relativities of historical enquiry with the absolute that faith needs? We can only do so as we distinguish between the standpoints peculiar to each. The first is that of the spectator, the disinterested observer, the second that of the responsible and committed participant. Life requires us to play now one now another of these rôles, and in each to profit by what we learned from the other. The first is concerned with what can be detached from the self and studied as an object. Its sphere is pre-eminently the past, though often only the past of a moment ago. The second is concerned with what impinges directly upon the self and challenges it. Its sphere is pre-eminently the present as that in which the shape of the future is to be decided. To the one corresponds the truth of information, one's knowledge is enlarged by it; to the other the truth of transformation, it leaves one a different person from what one was before. For the one, the 'absolute' is that which can be demonstrated to be free from anything that conditions it, and this cannot be found. There is no absolute for knowledge. For the other, the absolute is that which claims me personally here and now, puts my whole being under arrest. It is the absolute of Paul: 'Woe is me, if I preach not the gospel!' or Luther: '*Ich kann nicht anders.*'

The distinction is one with which the moral philosopher is familiar. The obligation to do one's duty is unconditional though admittedly all judgments as to what is in fact one's duty are conditioned by a variety of factors. In this way the historical becomes the vehicle of the absolute. 'The accent of eternity' falls upon a moment of time or, to use W. E. Hocking's phrase, a man may feel that the arc of destiny coincides with the swing of his arm. The absolute in such a situation is not that which has no part or lot with the relative, but that which is perfectly related, that which, in my present situation, I *must* do. Plato's *Apology* is the classic account of how a man can discern the absolute in the relative and be faithful to it. But this is matter of personal commitment arising out of personal discernment, and not something that can be demonstrated.

It is because he confuses these two standpoints that Mackintosh equates the finality of Christianity with the finality of Christ. But these are quite different. The first is an assertion about one set of historical phenomena in relation to other sets. The second is the acknowledgement of a person as adequate to all one's needs. Christ is absolute for me because, having him, I have all.

But is not this 'absolute for me' a dangerous expression? Can we be content with Troeltsch's language about 'God's countenance turned towards us'? In one sense, yes; in another sense, no. If there is anything in the argument so far, then the absolute of religion is necessarily an absolute 'for me' or, in the case of a community whose members share a common faith, an absolute 'for us'. But Troeltsch does not mean this. The tone in which he speaks—or writes—is one of regret, as though there were an absolute of a higher order that, unfortunately, is beyond our reach. But, as I have urged, there is no such absolute. If we are to see God at all, we must see him as he turns his face to us. We have a knowledge of the absolute but not absolute knowledge. In virtue of the first, we stand fast by the truth as we see it; in virtue of the second, we are open in love to the witness of others to the truth they have seen.

Von Hügel finds great difficulty in the concept of 'polymorphous truth' with which Troeltsch operates. How can I recognize the existence and right of truths other than my own and at the same time give entire devotion to my own truth? Troeltsch fails to solve this problem. For him, the recognition of other truths robs my own of something of its power. I must acquiesce in their existence with regret, since they throw doubt on my own truth. The most satisfactory discussion of this difficult problem is that of Karl Jaspers in his *Vernunft und Existenz*. There is no theoretical solution, but only an existential one. I must neither allow my own truth to sink to the level of one among many, as though it were mine merely by some personal preference, nor use it to destroy the right of others to live, each by the truth as he sees it. I must regard my neighbour's truth as challenge and opportunity. In open communication with him, I shall either (a) come to hold my truth more firmly, or (b) abandon it because I have seen that it is not true, or (c) recast it in the form of a fuller and richer truth. In either case, so long as my concern is for truth and not for my own opinion of it, I stand to gain. We may state this in another way by reverting to the distinction between the standpoints of the observer and the participant. The relation between the truth that is mine and the truth that is yours cannot be seen rightly on the plane of the observer, since for him neither is truth. He sees only conflicting claims thereto. On the plane of the participant, there is no truth save that to which I come under the guidance of God and in a relation of love to my fellows, that is to say, in openness to the truth by which you live. The obligation to follow the light I have is always accompanied by the obligation to seek after fuller light.

Criticism

f. CHRISTIANITY AS SUPERIOR

Now that we have dismissed the claim of Christianity to be absolute, what of the more modest suggestion that it is at any rate superior to other religions? Here, Troeltsch's argument seems to me unanswerable. Eucken's own treatment is a case in point. He denies, it will be remembered, that any actual religion can be absolute; the absolute religion, or characteristic religion as he calls it, is present in, with, and under the historical religions. But whence does he obtain this characteristic religion? As he himself admits, it is a construction based on Christianity. But is not such a construction valueless? Of course, Christianity will do better than its rivals in an examination at which it has set most of the questions! Toynbee confirms Troeltsch's judgment when he writes:

In our generation, there is not anyone alive who is effectively in a position to judge between his own religion and his neighbour's. An effective judgment is impossible when one is comparing a religion which has been familiar to one in one's home since one's childhood with a religion which one has learnt to know from outside in later years. One's ancestral religion is bound to have so much the stronger hold upon one's feelings that one's judgment between this and any other religion cannot be objective.[1]

Nor is this disproved by the case of the convert. For such a person is notoriously unreliable as a witness to the religion he has forsaken for another. He leaves it because it failed to satisfy, so that we cannot learn from him what it means to one for whom it is an adequate guide.

It would seem, therefore, that we cannot claim that Christianity is superior, if by this is meant some objective judgment on the religions. This does not mean that it is inferior, but simply that the language of superiority and inferiority is out of place in the sphere of religion, especially for the Christian. The religious

[1] *An Historian's Approach to Religion*, Oxford University Press, 1956, p. 296.

131

spirit knows nothing of any comparison between itself and others, but only of the humility that comes from measuring itself by the divine holiness. From the standpoint of faith, comparison is out of the question. He to whom worship if offered is not superior to others, he is incomparable. The moment we begin to compare, we exchange the standpoint of the believer for that of the observer. Even there, as we have seen, the question of superiority is decided in advance by the standard employed for the comparison.

Does this mean that no comparison between religions is possible? Are we shut up to a conflict between rival claims with no means of adjudicating between them? By no means. When it was said earlier that the standpoints of the observer and the participant must be distinguished, it was said also that neither is sufficient of itself. The commitment of faith must be subjected continually to the scrutiny and criticism of knowledge, lest it degenerate into wishful thinking or fanaticism. It must be exposed also, we have said, to the challenge of commitments in others that differ from one's own. What is personal and existential must in both cases be translated into concepts and propositions on which rational discourse can operate. If there is to be communication in truth and love between the representatives of the great religions—and it is towards this that we are moving—there must be argument at a rational level. The believer must achieve sufficient detachment to enable him to speak of his faith as something he observes and describes, yet not be so detached that the description ceases to convey what his faith means to him. The Christian, for example, will tell the Hindu why a faith that is rooted in history seems to him more adequate than one that appeals to general ideas, and the Hindu will reply. The Buddhist will state his objections to belief in a personal Creator and a permanent self and the Christian will defend his own position against his criticisms. Is there perhaps a parallel here to the arguments for God's existence? We believe in God, we cannot demonstrate him. But the traditional arguments and such new ones as we may bring forward are not therefore without value.

They express and confirm a faith in God that is already present, they make clear to those who do not share that faith what we believe and what we do not believe. So the personal confession 'I am a Christian' may be assisted and strengthened by setting out just how and where Christianity has that to offer which is not present in other faiths. But let me resist the temptation to pride that lurks in the use of such a word as 'superiority' in this connection.

XI

Towards a Conclusion

a. CONFLICT

ALL that we have seen so far goes to confirm our initial suspicion that the problem of the relation between the great religions is one that does not admit of an easy solution. The fact of conflict has emerged again and again, one religion repudiating what is as the breath of life to another. This takes its most overt form in the division of the world between a number of civilizations, each drawing its inspiration originally from a single religion or—in the case of China—a single philosophy. Our Western world is still nominally Christendom, as the Arab nations are bound to each other by Islam, while India, for all its Westernization, has still a culture of its own, based on Hinduism. Each of these civilizations has its own assumptions, its own thought-forms, its own standards of value, so that any effort to compare them is obstructed from the outset by the fact that there are no common standards that can be applied impartially. Each of us is committed to one or other of these patterns of culture. The sociologist will say that one may not ask whether Christian or Moslem marriage is better, but only whether each fulfils the rôle for which it is cast within its own society. If we wish to go beyond that, we must compare Islamic and Christian culture as two distinct wholes, each with its own claims.

But this should not be allowed to lead us to the despairing conclusion that the great religions occupy so many hermetically sealed compartments, so that communication between them is out of the question. This is the position reached by Troeltsch in his later study. But has he not carried the principle of individuality too far, making it in fact one of those absolutes he is concerned to deny? The various civilizations are not as starkly opposed as the analysis in the previous paragraph would suggest. To those who are not lacking in sympathy and imagination and can shake off prejudice, there are amazing possibilities of mutual under-standing on the part of people with diverse backgrounds. My own experience as one who has lived in the Far East and travelled in West Africa is that one has no sooner reached the conclusion that the mind of another people is a sealed book and that their standards are different from one's own than one discovers how much one has in common with them. Confucius and Mencius are some-times incomprehensible to a modern Englishman, sometimes nearer to him than the editorial in his morning paper. Those who have had fellowship at a deep level with adherents of another religion can no longer think of them as inhabitants of another intellectual and spiritual planet.

Again, granted the influence of geographical, racial, and cultural conditions upon a religion, is not this another reason for refusing to regard the individual character of each religion as an insurmountable barrier? For we are now in a period of large-scale intercourse and interaction. The New Testament is read in Japan and the Upanishads have their devotees in every Western country. The historical setting of every religion today is one of intellectual uncertainty, confusion even, and immense spiritual need. The future of each is at stake and therefore of humanity as a whole. We can no longer say that Christianity is 'final and unconditional for us, because we have nothing else'. Any claim we make for it today must be made in face of numerous counter-claims. The field is open for communication and common effort; we must think in global terms and no longer of civilizations so unique that they are sealed off from each other. Conflict is undoubted, but we may not accept it as final.

If now we consider the opposition that obtains at the purely religious level, we shall see it as fundamentally that between the three great Biblical religions and the religions of India. It is the clash between monotheism and monism, between the appeal to one God who is Creator and Lord of all and the quest of unity with an impersonal divine principle. This carries with it a grave difference in the evaluation of the world and history. Monotheism accepts the world as real, as having a definite origin and moving towards a definite termination at some future date; for monism it is *maya*, illusory, the present phase is a beginning-less and endless series of cycles. Monotheism takes pride in the fact that it has a historical basis, the exodus from Egypt, the crucifixion under Pontius Pilate, the Hegira: it reveres the personality of a founder. For the monisms, general philosophical ideas take the place of historical events. The Hindu doctrine of man is meta-psychological, a piece of subtle and—as it seems to us—unsubstantiated analysis; the Christian doctrine operates with such concepts as the image of God, responsibility and love. A comparison of the two is no more possible than a conversation between one who knows only English and another who has only Chinese.

But perhaps the most acute conflict has still to be mentioned. The Hinayana Buddhist may say that the difference between the way he follows and that taken by Jew, Christian, or Moslem is so great that he must deny that the word 'religion' is common to both. Buddhism, he will say, is not a religion at all. It acknowledges no God, but only gods who are caught, like men, in the net of karma; no future life, but only the bliss—or extinction—of Nirvana; no soul, but only the legacy of one life bequeathed to another that falls heir to it; no prayer, but only meditation as a form of spiritual discipline; no grace, but only man's resolve to tread the Noble Eight-Fold Path to the end. Could there be more serious conflict than this? How discuss the relation between the great religions when one of them informs us at the outset that it is not a religion at all? We seem to have arrived at the position stated so succinctly by Professor Zaehner in his inaugural lecture at Oxford. The religions differ, not because they give different answers to the same question, but because they ask different questions.

Towards a Conclusion

b. DIVERSITY

Is it possible to advance beyond this situation of conflict, as, for example, by reducing it to a clash of insights, each partial indeed but each in its place legitimate? Toynbee makes just this attempt in his *Study of History*. His approach is a psychological one. He fastens on the phenomenon of compensation as his starting-point. An individual who carries his development too far in one direction thereby does injury to his personality as a whole. But this brings with it its own remedy, as the psyche sets up in the unconscious a tendency that goes to redress the balance. The hard-headed employer may be soft-hearted within the family, the intellectual turns to crime-fiction for diversion, and so on. So it is with a religion. It tends to stress one aspect of the truth and neglect others. Sooner or later this calls into being a counter-movement, which in turns goes too far, so that once again a compensatory movement is called for. A Catholicism that allows Christ to become obscured by the Virgin provokes a Protestant reaction; this proves too masculine, and Anglo-Catholicism revives features of the old tradition. In India the dominant *advaita* fails to satisfy and in the *bhakti* cults men turn in devotion to a personal God.

Perhaps what obtains within each religion may also obtain between the religions. Each of them is able to meet certain deep needs of the soul, but only at the cost of leaving others unsatisfied. The compensatory movement thus called into being leads to some degree of borrowing from another's store. Syncretism is inescapable in practice, even where frowned upon in theory. If Catholicism takes over the Mother-Goddess of paganism to satisfy the craving for a feminine object of worship, Protestantism is deeply indebted to the synagogue. In spite of the claim of some religions to possess the final truth, their history is a confession that they do not cover the whole range of human needs. The fullness of truth does not lie with one of them but is spread over all.

But how is it so spread? Here Toynbee has recourse to Jung's classification of psychological types. There is first the contrast

between the extrovert whose attention is fastened on the outside
world and the introvert whose eye is turned within. Then we
have the four basic functions of thought and feeling, sensation
and intuition, to be taken thus in pairs. Without forcing a system
upon the variety of individuals, we can construct a series of types
that will serve as guides to an understanding of that variety.
In any person, one of the four functions will play a dominant
part; as a consequence of this, the other member of the pair will
tend to be repressed. The remaining two functions will be used as
auxiliaries or also repressed—no rule can be laid down, for it is
here that individual differences come into play. To illustrate, the
intellectual will tend to be deficient in the emotional side of his
life; how sensation and intuition enter into his make-up will vary
from case to case. Finally, the repressed function will probably
not allow itself to be relegated to the unconscious once for all; it
will break out from time to time and manifest itself in more or
less disturbing fashion.

It only remains to apply this scheme to the great religions.
Judaism, Christianity, and Islam are extrovert because they
worship a personal God who created the world and is at work in
history. Hinduism and Buddhism are introvert, because for them
the divine is within, the dweller in the innermost. Again, the
dominant function in Hinduism is thought, in Islam feeling, and
in Buddhism intuition. Thus each has appeal and validity as
meeting the needs of some psychological type.

It will be sufficient to indicate very briefly the further steps
in the analysis. In Hinduism thinking dominates, we saw; this
is associated with sensation and intuition, which find expression
respectively in ritual and yoga. Feeling, banished to the unconscious, forces its way to the light in the *bhakti* cults. In Christianity
feeling is dominant and thinking repressed; for, while Christianity
has always had its intellectuals, they have been employed in the
service of the Church and its dogmas, not set free, as in India.
Intuition is found in the mystics and sensation in ritual. In Islam
sensation is dominant and thinking is associated with it; feeling
comes to its own in the Shi'ah, and intuition forces its way in as

Sufi mysticism. Finally, Buddhism is primarily a religion of intuition, and this co-operates with thought in the Hinayana and with feeling in the Mahayana. Sensation could not be entirely repressed, and avenges itself in such practices as the worship of relics.

On a strictly psychological theory this is as far as we have a right to go. Each type must be accepted as ultimate, no gradation or comparison being possible.

The divers higher religions must resign themselves to playing limited parts, and must school themselves to playing these parts in harmony, in order, between them, to fulfil their common purpose of enabling every human being or every psychological type to enter into communion with God the Ultimate Reality.[1]

But Toynbee cannot be content merely to classify, he must go on to judge. Man's chief end, he tells us, is to glorify God and enjoy him for ever, and he does this by feeling rather than by thought.

On this showing, the most valuable instruments in the orchestra of Religion would be those that played the music of Love; and, on an order of merit determined by that criterion, Christianity would head the list.[2]

Next to it come Shi'ah Islam and Mahayana Buddhism, with Hinduism at the foot of the list. The last-named has, however, one excellence lacking in Christianity. It is tolerant and comprehensive, unwilling to outlaw any religion that brings man help and strength.

In this argument, as Toynbee frankly admits, a Christian conclusion is reached because the premises are Christian. A Hindu might well complain that the verdict has gone against him only because the jury was packed. Once again we see that in these high matters there is no imparital perspective, that we take our stand on what Troeltsch called the 'fine point of personal conviction'.

[1] Op. cit. vii. 734.   [2] Ibid. p. 735.

To return from this digression to the theory of types. At first sight, it is unquestionably attractive, but closer examination suggests that it is one of those brilliant generalizations that are suggestive rather than convincing. I confine myself to one criticism that may serve to advance the argument a stage further. Are we really to suppose that the four main psychological types have been distributed somehow over the earth's surface so that one prevails in the Far East, a second in the Near and Middle East, and a third in Europe and America? All experience goes to show the contrary. Christianity, for example, includes a number of great churches and small sects, each of which has tensions within itself, parties differing in outlook, congregations many of which have a peculiar ethos, and so on. It does not seem to be otherwise with the other great religions. Each of them is able to maintain its authority over great masses of men in virtue, in part at least, of its ability to cater for the needs of the whole gamut of psychological types. This suggests that we should look to some theory of types—not necessarily Jung's—not to explain the diversity of the religions, but to establish affinities between them.

c. AFFINITY

The question I propose to ask in this section runs: Is there perhaps a classification by types that cuts across the classification by religions, so that a particular type can be traced in several religions? If so, there would be a measure of affinity between them.

H. N. Spalding, in his survey of *Civilization in East and West*, may serve as guide at this point. He enumerates four types of state or, as it would be better to say, society. The first is that of primitive man, the 'biological society'. From this, man sets out on the long pilgrimage of reason and arrives first at the 'materialist society'. Here interest is still focused on the world, concerns are practical, and man is in the centre of the picture. By contrast the 'moral-spiritual society' looks towards God, conceives him as personal, and seeks reconciliation with him. Finally, in the 'spiritual society' the claims of this world yield to those of the other, the dominant mood is one of contemplation, and man yearns after unity with the divine as the end of his being.

As the argument develops, Spalding tends to set Indian religion at the climax of the process and assimilate Christianity to it. I am not concerned here with this or other features of his argument. What is of value is that, in allocating one or more of the non-Christian religions to each form of post-primitive society, he sets beside it one of the three major types of Christianity. There is thus a link between Orthodoxy, Catholicism, and Protestantism and at least one non-Christian religion in each case. Let us see how this is worked out.

To the moral society Spalding assigns Chinese religion with the Confucian strain predominant in it. The parallel to this is not Protestantism as such, but the version of it current among the busy, practical nations of northern Europe. The moral-spiritual society is represented by Israel and Islam on the one hand and by Catholicism on the other. In all three, God's law is the source of moral obligation, and man relates himself to God by obedience or submission or dependence on his grace. The spiritual society is the work of Hinduism and Buddhism in one hemisphere and of Orthodoxy in the other. For the latter is strongly influenced by Neoplatonism and shares with the mystics of all ages a belief in the divine element within the soul. The salvation it offers is *theosis*, the deification of man and nature. As Keyserling puts it: 'In order to be pious in the Indian sense one has either to be born an Indian or a Russian.'[1]

There is much truth in this analysis, but one important modification is called for. The great religions are too complex for the relations between them to be as simple as is here made out. It is clear, for example, that Catholicism has as much in common with Hinduism as with Islam, if not more. We must establish affinities, not between the religions as such, but between the patterns of spiritual experience that may be identified within them. So, for example, Orthodoxy will be akin to Hinduism in

[1] *Travel Diary*, p. 226.

virtue of feature A and to Islam in virtue of feature B; Lutheranism will stretch out a hand to one form of Buddhism but not to others, and so on. The religions, that is to say, are like cities, each of which has within it a group of people related by kinship to the people of other cities. While they retain their loyalty unimpaired, they can therefore interpret to their rulers the policies of those other cities and so make friendship possible where otherwise hostility would threaten.

So, in *Truth and Revelation*, Berdyaev at times confesses himself more in sympathy with Indian thought than with that of Western Christianity. Its concept of the divine is not so crudely personal nor so harshly judicial and authoritarian; it treads the *via negativa*, more ready to say what God is not than what he is. Its concept of man is more generous, and it is not disposed to condemn multitudes to the flames of hell. No Calvinist should listen to those who accuse the Koran of teaching fatalism. He, like the Moslem, attempts to combine God's predestination with man's freedom and responsibility. Illogical this may be, but who can doubt its power in history? Every observer of the Jodo and Shinshu sects of Buddhism in Japan has been struck by their likeness to Lutheranism—the same emphasis on salvation by faith and not by works, the same entry of the religious life into the secular calling. Did not Shinran marry, as Luther did, in the name of the latter principle? Some of the hymns sung in the services of these two sects would need little adaption for use in Methodist worship. What religion has not had its controversies over reason and revelation? The effort to return to the historical Jesus had had its parallel in the call 'Back to Buddha'. There have been Christian theologians who would have been thoroughly at home in the dispute among Vaishnavites as to whether God's grace saves us as a cat carries its kittens or as a monkey carries its young. One could wish, indeed, that Western theology had conducted its debates in such language. And even so no mention has been made of the most striking case of affinity, that of mysticism in all its forms. Here the quest is one and the goal, when it is reached, is one.

d. UNITY

The considerations brought forward in the previous section makes it possible to hope for a measure of unity. Yet it must be a unity that includes within it tension and conflict, even the rejection by one religion of that which is precious to another. Perhaps what obtains within Christianity itself may help us to see what might be possible over a wider area. The ecumenical movement has led the churches to the paradoxical position in which their divisions are more sharply defined than before, because they have been brought out into the open and clearly formulated, and yet they are aware as never before that Christian unity is a reality. On certain points, such as the ministry and the sacraments, we seem to be confronted by insuperable difficulties; we know now that we are divided by basic convictions and not merely by prejudices. Yet for all that we can no longer be indifferent to each other, as we once were. We are drawn together, we learn from each other, we recognize each other as servants of the same Lord—yet we cannot sit together at the communion table. There is unity in spirit even where any attempt to express this unity divides us. To be sincere, we must use our own words, and they constitute a barrier at once. Yet this unity of the spirit is no vague and misty thing; it is something by which we are learning to live. Perhaps it is only in silent worship and practical collaboration on particular projects than we can grasp our unity as a reality.

Perhaps it is even so with the great religions. Just as the Protestant may be conscious at once of his unity with a Catholic friend at the level of prayer and worship and of his conflict with him at the level of theology, so Christian and Hindu may be drawn together in the life of the spirit yet separate when they put into words what that life is for them. Between the wars, during a short stay in Japan, I visited the community of Ittoen near Kyoto and met its founder and head, Tenko Nishida. Though a Buddhist, he had been deeply influenced by Tolstoi and the New Testament. The hour I spent in conversation with him was a most moving and memorable experience, though again and again there was much in what he said that I was prepared to challenge. After our conversation I slipped away to the shrine of the brotherhood, kept for private worship. It was in two parts. One contained a Shinto tablet, a small figure of Buddha, and a cross. In the other was a simple lamp burning the rape-seed oil a peasant uses, and kept alight continually. Each person who worshipped there was free to choose the symbol he preferred, that which was peculiar to his own faith or that which stood for their underlying unity, the Light that lighteneth every man that cometh into the world. As I knelt before that lamp, I too entered into that unity of the spirit which did not abolish our several allegiances even while it transcended them.

XII

Communication

a. RECONCEPTION

OUR discussion thus far has brought us to the point reached by W. E. Hocking in his *Living Religions and a World Faith*. The religions may not be dissolved into general ideas, their strength lies to no small extent in what marks them off from each other. 'The price of existence must be paid. We shall not arrive at the world faith by omitting the particulars.'[1] The religions of the East are not religions in the same sense as Christianity, so comparison between them is difficult, if indeed it is legitimate. Each, again, is highly complex, so that our attempts to define it never do justice to it. Most of our criticisms of a religion other than our own are invalid for the simple reason that it is one thing for those who live by it and another for those who do not. We turn aside attacks on Christianity by pleading that they are valid only against 'empirical', not against 'genuine', Christianity. But what is to prevent a Buddhist from urging that Buddhism has not failed, it has been found difficult and not tried? Further, the religions of the East are not defunct, they are taking on new forms to meet the challenge of the modern world. We allow that such a procedure is legitimate in our own case, but seem to regard it as unfair when, say, Islam follows our example. We want to stereotype the other religions so that we can always feel superior to them. They ought to stagnate and die. But they refuse to oblige us. We must allow a religion to be what its followers claim that it is.

[1] Op. cit. 1940, p. 57.

Hocking then goes on to consider the possibility of a world faith emerging one day and what the prospects are of Christianity becoming such a faith. There are three paths to this goal. The first is that of *radical displacement*, one religion aiming to supersede all others. The second is that of *synthesis*, the inclusion within one's religion of what is good in the others. If the first errs by bigotry, the second does so by weakness. It neglects the distinction between truth and error. Of course, we must be willing to learn from each other. But let us take nothing over save as it convinces us of its truth. We may say that syncretism is permissible so long as it is not a deliberate policy but comes about naturally as men of open mind share their experiences.

What Hocking himself advocates is *reconception*. Let the representatives of each religion look at once without and within. Challenged as they are by one another, let each use the knowledge he has of the others to enable him to understand his own religion better, to penetrate beyond the adventitious to the essential. As we see our own religion through the eyes of those who are of a different allegiance, we shall learn to distinguish what is vital and primary in it from what is merely traditional and secondary.

One's conceptions have been inadequate; they have not anticipated these new vistas and motives: we require to understand our own religion better—we must *reconceive it*—then we shall see how the new perspectives belong quite naturally to what has always been present in its nature, unnoticed or unappreciated by us.[1]

By such a process, the religions will be drawn together in mutual understanding. The return of each to its essence will be the return of all together to what they have in common. Not that in the process they will be reduced to the same terms, to a few simple ideas: what is local and particular must live on. But could there not be a rivalry between religions, not to win converts, but to reach truth and serve mankind? We may therefore look for 'a growing resemblance among religions', but there will be

[1] Op. cit. 1940, pp. 191 f.

'no immediate tendency to diminish the number of particular religions'.

Nevertheless, the process *does tend to a decision*, not through a conflict of faiths or a campaign for world dominance, but through the unforced persuasiveness of relative success in this effort to become a better vehicle of truth.[1]

I suspect that my quarrel with Hocking is over his language rather than over the intention behind it. I am not happy about the use of the term 'essence' in this connection. Again, such a word as 'reconception' suggests something less than the unreserved openness to the challenge of another faith that I would wish to see. The experience of the ecumenical movement suggests that the danger that one will merely be confirmed in one's original position is a serious one. Also, to enter into conversation on the assumption that 'the new perspectives' will be seen to 'belong quite naturally to what has always been present', albeit 'unnoticed or unappreciated by us', is to ensure that the danger will not be avoided. In the later book *The Coming World Civilization* Hocking makes it clearer that he has in mind a process of assimilation that is consistent with fidelity to one's own truth. But he still falls short of the complete exposure and total risk that are involved in such a full and frank encounter as alone can assure that truth is advanced thereby. I find him too optimistic in his judgment that Christianity has by now achieved sufficient freedom from Western civilization and its peculiarities to qualify it for taking 'a certain leadership in meeting the religious problems of the coming civilization'.[2]

For 'reconception' I would therefore substitute 'communication' in the sense the word bears in Karl Jaspers's philosophy.

Is the only unity truly obtainable to us humans unity through communication of the historically manifold origins, which are mutually concerned with one another, without becoming identical in the manifestation of idea and symbol—a unity which leaves the One concealed

[1] Op. cit. 1940, p. 201. [2] Op. cit. 1956, p. 136.

in manifoldness, the One that can remain true only in the will to boundless communication, as an endless task in the interminable testing of human possibilities? [1]

'The will to boundless communication'—is not this what is needed?

b. CONFLICT OF TRUTHS

In the relation between the religions, conflict, as we have seen, is inescapable. If they sometimes agree, they also often differ, and there are occasions when they seem irreconcilably opposed. But the situation is even more complex than it has been presented hitherto. For sometimes, just where the affinity is greatest, divergence reveals itself. A few instances of this will suffice. I have adverted to the 'Lutheranism' of the Jodo and Shinshu sects in Japan. They preach salvation by faith, but not as the one possibility for sinning man; it is the 'easy way' that is opened in this degenerate age. They proclaim a Saviour and his grace, but they acknowledge that he never actually lived; he is symbol and myth. Buddhist compassion prompts to the same actions as Christian love, but they differ profoundly in their metaphysical basis. The Christian loves his neighbour because he is other than himself, a person with unique rights that must be respected; the Buddhist loves his neighbour because he is *not* other than himself, since all life is one and the self is unreal in all. Ramanuja knows of a God of love who created the world; but that world is not unique, with a beginning and an end, it is one phase of a process that is endlessly repetitive. How shall we describe such cases? Is the conflict uppermost or the unity?

The presupposition of communication is that, here and elsewhere, no one party to the debate has a monopoly of the truth. Each can lay claim to no more than a partial glimpse of it, so that the one hope of advancing beyond this to a larger insight

[1] *The Origin and Goal of History*, London: Routledge & Kegan Paul, 1949, p. 264.

is by the willingness to meet and learn from each other. What has laid hold upon me must neither be lightly surrendered nor obstinately adhered to. It must be exposed to the challenge and criticism of what has similarly laid hold upon you. Conflict there must be, but it will be a conflict waged in love, each seeking victory not for himself but for a truth that will be common to both and will bind them together. The opponent in each case is not the other person, but the ignorance, the prejudice, the self-satisfaction within oneself that prevent growth. But for such a relation the first requisite is complete openness. Everything must be brought out into the light of day; nothing must be kept back because it is too dear to be surrendered even were it proved false. Meanwhile, we are supported by a common faith in truth as the pearl of great price for which it were well worth while to sell all that we have and are up to this point.

All that can be done at present is to call for this boundless communication. What will come out of it we cannot foresee. No syncretism, no assimilation, no world faith is envisaged, but something better than these—a growth in mutual understanding, and a participation in the life of the spirit at a level where words and definitions break down. In the language of George Fox, we 'shall meet and know one another in that which is eternal'. It is the paradoxical nature of such communication that it must present in arguments that which arguments cannot touch, must throw into the form of rational discourse that which can be known but not defined. For we can only share in spiritual experience as we put it into words, employ concepts, and state our own point of view over against another's. The two extremes to be avoided are, first, the withdrawal of each party to the conversation into a realm of private feeling, and second, the reduction of intense and personal experiences to abstract ideas. He who has genuinely shared with a person of another faith knows how difficult it is to avoid these two pitfalls, but he knows also that it can be done.

Perhaps I may be permitted to make three brief contributions here to such communication from the Christian side. It is a commonplace among Christian theologians that, as Tillich puts it, all our statements about God—with the single exception of this statement, which after all is only indirectly about him—are symbolic. There is as yet little disposition to admit that this is the case with the non-Christian religions. The Upanishads and the Koran are to be taken literally, the New Testament symbolically! But is this fair? Once grant that all our language about God is a pointer to that which no language can express, it may well be that we need two sets of symbols if we are not to fail entirely in our speech of him. The West experiences the Transcendent as a personal God, the East as an impersonal divine principle. That neither of these is absolute is shown by the fact that, on the one hand, Christian theology is forced at times to speak of 'ultimate reality' and 'the nature of things', and that, on the other, the soul of India has again and again turned in loving devotion to God as personal. Perhaps that is dominant for the one which is subordinate in the other.

This leads to the second point. Is an understanding between monism and monotheism possible? Or, we may ask whether each can do justice to the other. For monism, of course, the worship of Isvara, the personal Creator and Lord, belongs to the relative world, the sphere of ignorance, of transmigration and salvation. Monism, as it were, includes monotheism within it as a particular case, just as the theory of relativity includes Newtonian physics. I think that it is possible for monotheism in its turn to include monism within it. The static world-view of monism is, so to speak, a cross-section of the dynamic world-view of monotheism. If God maintains the world in being from moment to moment by an activity that presents each situation with a possibility of redemption, so that God, as it were, adds to each phase of its development just that complement that would bring it to perfection, if accepted, then, could we arrest the process at one instant, we should see it as a perfect whole in which all evil was made the occasion of a greater good, and one's highest aim would be to merge oneself in that whole at the point where one's individuality entered it, and so to become one with the divine. The impersonal absolute of one system is the living-God-and-the-world-in-interrelation of the other system.

Finally, I would suggest how a Christian can view the anomaly of Hinayana, a religion that denies that it is a religion. For if our definition of religion is such that it excludes Buddhism, the inference to draw from this is that we must find another definition, or maybe decide that here is something that resists all attempts at definition. Perhaps we should think of God as revealing himself to men in two ways. In one, he offers himself as a gift to be received; in the other, he holds himself in reserve as a prize to be won. So, in the teaching of Jesus, the kingdom of God is now something to be reached in the spirit of a little child, now something only for him who is willing to take up the cross and bear it after Jesus. For Paul, the man who surrenders all claims of his own must at the same time be pictured as straining every nerve to reach the goal and win the prize. Karl Jaspers speaks of 'the reticence of God'. He remains silent, stays in the background, throws us on our own resources, because he cares so much for us. If then for Christianity God is known primarily as gift, this is not to say that there are not those, as in Buddhism, by whom he wills to be won as prize. Once again, God is too great to be apprehended exclusively through one set of symbols. Two sets are needed, and these in apparent conflict. If they are after all not so much opposed as complementary, it is only in communication that this can be seen.

c. LEVELS OF DECISION

Such communication as is here called for is in fact no new thing. Wherever the ecumenical movement has gone, it has become part of the daily life of the churches. It is by the combination of fidelity to one's historic witness with openness to the witness of others that they have come to a fuller understanding of their unity in Christ. Where such openness is refused, on the ground that one already has the truth and that nothing remains to be learned, communication is impossible and unity is not achieved.

Let us bring out by an example the sort of thing that has happened again and again. The convinced Protestant, coming to a better knowledge of Roman Catholicism or Greek Orthodoxy, finds himself taking up four attitudes to it.

(*a*) He discovers it in the truth he already holds, so that to this extent unity is already present.

(*b*) He finds in it that which he must reject as error. To this extent conflict must continue, but it can be qualified by charity.

(*c*) He finds in it that which appeals to him as a new truth, some idea or practice hitherto strange to him which convinces him as something he must learn and make his own.

(*d*) He finds it in that which he can neither accept as truth nor dismiss as error. He realizes its spiritual value for others but it does not speak to his condition. He must respect it, but he cannot make it his own.

I suggest that communication between the great religions may well have the same outcome. The first of the four attitudes presents no difficulty and calls for no comment. I shall therefore illustrate briefly the other three.

(*a*) For the foreseeable future, conflict must be accepted as inescapable. Each of the great religions sees that in the others which it must reject, and nothing is to be gained by concealing this unpleasant fact. As a man who cannot say 'No' is without character, so a religion that cannot say 'No' is without power. As regards the application of this, I can only speak for myself. I appreciate the fact that the Moslem is under an obligation to speak no evil of the founders of other religions, and I am sure that we should reciprocate by refraining from the criticisms of Mohammed that come so easily. But I cannot regard Mohammed as a prophet in the same sense as Jeremiah and Second Isaiah. I am fully aware that a thoughtful Hindu finds the use of images in worship not incompatible with the unity and spirituality of God, as also that he may employ the language of sexual licence to express the soul's purest devotion: but to both these practices I find myself compelled to say 'No'. Whatever the future holds, the present leaves us in opposition on certain points. I do not doubt that the

Buddhist and the Hindu will wish to dissent in the same way from certain features in our Christianity.

(*c*) On the question of what the Christian may well learn from other religions, I find myself largely in agreement with Hocking. I add a few comments of my own. Are we Christians as sound as we think we are on the unity of God? I could wish that something like the muezzin's cry to prayer might ring out five times a day over our great cities in the West, calling its population to remember how all life is under the rule and mercy of one good, great God. Some even among our professional theologians might well go to school with the Moslem on this point. The tendency of the Christian moralist to abdicate before the necessities of the political struggle is in sharp contrast to the Confucian affirmation that justice and humanity must always take precedence of expediency, even in affairs of state. When I read in the Upanishads of the soul's quest for unity with the divine, I cannot doubt that there is here a genuine spiritual experience, and I long to enter into it for myself.

The judgment of two men with much greater experience than my own may be of value. The first was a missionary to India. He was once describing to a student audience in England how he went to that country only to teach, but found that he had also much to learn. One of his audience put the question to him: 'You say that we should be willing to learn from Indian religion. Give us one instance of what you have in mind.' He lowered his voice as he replied: 'The love of God for his own sake, and not for anything he gives.' The second was a missionary in Hong Kong, previously resident in China, who knew Chinese Buddhism from within as no other European of his day did. When a similar question was put to him, he replied: 'A sense of the immensities of space and time that are at God's disposal for his work, so that we are delivered from the so-much-to-do-so-little-done anxiety of the West.' Are not both these lessons well worth learning? I have spoken already of the striking contrast between the two imperial patrons, Asoka of Buddhism and Constantine of Christianity. If only we could learn from the religions of the

East their patience and tolerance that put to shame our lack of charity at the point where we profess it most! We need to take to heart the charge that Jaspers brings against us, that the Christian claim to possess absolute truth is in part responsible for the political and national fanaticisms of today.

(*d*) What is the Christian to think of Gautama Buddha, his struggle for truth, his enlightenment, and the message he has left behind him for the guidance of multitudes? What is he to think of the great and gracious souls nourished on Buddhism, the boundless devotion and self-abnegation of Santi-deva, the nobility of Prince Shotoku, the saints of Zen and the evangelists of Jodo? The presuppositions of this religion are not his own, it does not answer his questions, and it asks questions that are not his. He cannot say with it that 'all life is suffering', and he cannot with it equate the self with selfishness. That it is not the truth for him is clear. But can he deny that it has been the truth for multitudes of others? Neither acceptance nor rejection, it seems to me, does justice to the situation here. Here is something that I salute with profound respect, though I can never make it my own. Though not turned towards me, it may yet be the countenance of God. I cannot say 'Yes', nor can I say 'No'. I say rather: 'Here are depths in the wisdom of God that must be further explored.'

c. CHRIST LATENT AND MANIFEST

The title of this book requires that one final question be asked and answered: 'What, in the process of boundless communication here envisaged, are the prospects of Christianity?' Here, as was said earlier 'the conclusion at which one arrives in this matter is largely decided in advance by one's conception of Christianity'. What follows is therefore in the nature of a personal confession. But in this confession I am not alone.

The time is ripe for that radical reconception of which we have spoken, whereby the concept of the Christ is extended to include that unbound Spirit who stands at the door of every man, and who, in various guises, still appears to him who opens, both as an impersonal word and as personal presence.[1]

The Christian can enter into conversation with men and women of another faith because his aim in this is not to win them for his religion, but to serve that kingdom of Christ whose triumphs are only those of truth and love. He is willing to receive into the fellowship of the church all who would confess Christ by name; indeed, he invites them to enter it. But he does not demand that all become Christians. For he knows that Christendom has so sadly misinterpreted Christ that he may draw some to himself within their own religions as he could not do by gaining them for ours.

When '*In hoc signo*' ceases to be a battle cry, it will ascend as token of another conquest, the conquest of estrangement among the seekers of God.[2]

I would accept the thesis of the latent and the manifest Christ, as it is found in Sebastian Franck and Schelling. But I would add one important qualification. To neither form of Christ do we have access directly, but only in and through historically conditioned religions, of which Christianity is one. We may not therefore assume that, as Christians, we possess the key to the understanding of the non-Christian faiths, the criterion by which to distinguish truth from error in them. We know the manifest Christ only in part, so that we are not in a position to define the outlines of the latent Christ. The complete Christ, it may be, includes a glory in the latent Christ that waits to be recognized and appropriated by those who know him only as manifest. The faith that he is present in Christian and non-Christian alike should lead to frank conversation between the two, in the hope thereby to draw nearer to the complete Christ. Perhaps the time has come to restore to honour one of the oldest and most neglected symbols of the faith. We look for the Christ who is to come.

[1] *The Coming World Civilization*, London: Allen & Unwin, 1958, p. 169.
[2] *Living Religions*, London: Bailey Bros., 1956, p. 269.

Index

157

GEORGE ALLEN & UNWIN LTD
London: 40 Museum Street, W.C.1

Auckland: 24 Wyndham Street
Bombay: 15 Graham Road, Ballard Estate, Bombay 1
Calcutta: 17 Chittaranjan Avenue, Calcutta 13
Cape Town: 109 Long Street
Karachi: Metherson's Estate, Wood Street, Karachi 2
New Delhi: 13-14 Ajmeri Gate Extension, New Delhi 1
Sao Paulo: Avenida 9 de Julho 1138-Ap. 51
Singapore, South East Asia and the Far East: 36c Prinsep Street
Sydney, N.S.W.: Bradbury House, 55 York Street
Toronto: 91 Wellington Street West